High School

to

Heaven

∞ ∞

Joyce Glynn

Foremost, thank you to my immediate family - Roger, Amber and Matt - for patiently waiting for me to find my purpose, and for your support in this venture;

To Jim and Bob, who helped us form and implement the Michael Glynn Memorial Coalition;

To Tim and Marie - words can't describe the appreciation I have for the emotional help you have given me, all while journeying through your own time of grief;

To Charlotte - Michael's book is now finished!

And finally, thank you to my parents for the spiritual foundation you gave me as a child. Without it, we would be lost.

Preface

I apologize, in advance, for writing as I speak. Therefore, throughout the following pages, you will likely encounter a few grammar errors. This book is the true and honest account, in my words, of my feelings and emotions during the months following our son's death from an alcohol-related car crash the morning after his high school graduation.

You might notice that I use the word "crash" here, but in most instances of my journaling, I had used the term "accident." Insight into the effects of alcohol have taught me that it was very much a crash, rather an accident. This "crash" could have been prevented.

The purpose of journaling began as a form of personal therapy – a way to release the grief I was experiencing. Formatting my journal into this book, is not to seek sympathy or pity.

I have two goals:

One – that a young person will read this, and think to themselves, "I have goals for my future, and I don't want anything like alcohol to come between me and them, and I don't want to do anything that could cause my family to go through the pain of losing me." And,

Two – that a parent will read this, and think to themselves, "I love my children and want them to have a long, happy future. I am going to talk to them today, and often, about making the right choice when it comes to alcohol use. And I will lead them by my example. I do not want to become a member of "the club."

From birth on, there is a socially accepted order to our lives. We are born and raised by our parents, go through elementary and high school, continue our education or find a job or career, marry, have children, watch our children grow and give us grandchildren, then grieve at the death of our own parents. We prepare for our retirement and golden years, and know that some day our children will grieve as they bury us and we return to our home in Heaven. And the wheel continues to turn in the circle of our lives.

Our family's wheel was broken when Michael died. People tell us that "he's in a better place now." While I agree, it's not supposed to happen that way. He missed out on so many wonderful aspects of life here on earth! His death was preventable. The order of his life should not have been, from High School to Heaven.

Preface

As is the same on many late nights, I sit here at my computer, mindlessly surfing and wasting time. My searches always end up taking the same route, even though I try to not go there. I search the name – Michael Glynn.

Of course, I know my Michael Glynn. I search for others now, who share his name. I look for resemblances, or similarities. I find none. No one can take his place.

From the moment of birth, sometimes while even in the womb, everyone believes their child is the cutest, the smartest, the most talented, the best at "whatever." I guess I'm no exception to that rule either. Michael was a very wanted baby. He was the first little Glynn baby to be born at our ranch in over 30 years.

Roger's grandfather's name was Mike Glynn. He was a mean and ornery cuss to many. But to Roger and his brothers, he was an icon. He must have loved his grandchildren dearly, for Roger isn't one to show much admiration to many; but he did to his Grandpa Glynn.

When we found out I was expecting a baby, Roger was ecstatic, as was his mother. She had been waiting for Roger to marry and start a family for many years! She often said she couldn't hardly wait to have a little grand-baby next door that she could watch over and coddle.

As soon as we found out the baby would be a boy, his name was decided. Roger insisted his first son be named after his grandfather – Mike. He wanted his boy to grow up strong and wise, just as his great-grandfather – and dedicated to the family heritage of a strong love of the land and livestock. Who wouldn't want that for their child? After Michael's birth, I even wrote in his baby book that we hoped someday he would end up raising his family on the family ranch – the ranch started by his great-grandfather, his namesake, Mike Glynn.

So it was set. Michael's future had begun the day he was born – August 7, 1987.

Michael was a beautiful little baby. He had the biggest, brownest eyes, and the longest eye lashes. I used to joke with him that he would have made a beautiful little girl! And he would have! But there was no "girl" in him. He was all boy! He was a rough and tumble little guy, right from the start.

Michael loved all things outdoors. He would follow his dad and grandpa all day long. When Roger was too busy, or doing something too dangerous for the kids to be with him, grandpa would step in. He was never too busy when it came to his grandkids.

When Michael was about 3 years old, grandpa sat him on top of his horse when he led him across the road to the corral one evening. When they got to the gate, the horse jumped a little, and Michael went off, right into the soft grass and mud. Never the less, the fall shied him from horses. That almost broke grandpa's heart. He felt so bad. Michael wanted nothing to do with horses for quite some time after that.

Almost two years later, Roger found a saddle horse that a neighbor had for sale. The horse wasn't much to look at, really. It was black with a white spot on his forehead. But he wasn't a very big horse, he was very gentle, and Mikey fell in love with him. Stormy came home from the sale the next week, and Mikey's attitude about horses changed drastically. Immediately, he was riding every day, and the two developed a strong bond. Never again did he show any fear around any animal. Deep respect – yes, but never fear. As a young teenager, Michael was the only one Roger would let ride his own saddle horses. Partly because he knew Michael wouldn't spoil the horse and allow him to have bad habits, and also because he knew Michael could handle himself on any mount.

By the time Michael was seven years old, he was wanting to ride anything, and everything. He became infatuated with rodeos. So, we took him to some little jack-pot rodeos where he started riding calves. Soon, when he was old enough, he moved up the ranks to steers in 4-H and Little Britches rodeos. It wasn't long, then, until he found his true love in rodeo – riding bulls.

Now, I didn't grow up in a ranching, much less a rodeo, family. So this was all new to me. I remember the times he would get bucked off a little yearling bull or steer, and I would go running to the fence to make sure he was ok and get the dirt wiped off his britches. He was appalled! One time I did that at a rodeo when he was probably 10 or 11 years old, because I really was worried that he had gotten stepped on. Well, he was fine. In fact, he was so fine, that he refused to talk to me all the way home that night. According to him, I had embarrassed him beyond acceptance! I mean, what self-respecting bull rider has his mommy follow him to the back of the chutes to make sure he doesn't have an owie?

Michael had been horrified at my behavior, and even Roger thought I was being way too over-protective. So, as he learned to ride bulls, I learned to stay sitting in the bleachers. Our compromise was that I would take him to official bull riding schools, where he would learn to ride, not only well, but safely, and he would let me go check on him only if someone else thought he really was hurt.

We spent countless hours on the road with Michael then, as he pursued his dream of rodeo. As he became better, and gained confidence in himself while growing up, I too gained confidence in his abilities, and grew up some myself.

I remember once when he got bucked off and just laid there for a second, someone next to me asked how I could let him participate in such a dangerous sport. This woman couldn't imagine me watching him ride bulls, then doing nothing when he was on the ground afterward. I remember telling her that after a while you don't worry so much. When you watch your kids doing what they absolutely love, you simply leave it in the hands of God. I also remember telling her that I worried more about him playing football, than riding bulls. To explain – when riding a bull, the bull only wants to buck him off. If all goes well it only lasts eight seconds, and there are many people in the arena to protect him. In a football game – it lasts more than an hour, and there are nine other kids his size and larger, wanting to seriously hurt him!

I could go on and on with stories about Michael's early childhood, but really, they're not that unique. Michael was pretty much an ordinary all-around kid. Stories about him and his escapades could be echoed by many, many parents and their children.

The difference now rests, as does Michael's body, in a cemetery.

To say that Michael had a wild side while in high school was probably an under statement. He was daring and carefree. He lived for the moment, and filled each with as much fun as he could muster.

And yes, there came a time when we knew he had started drinking alcohol.

As many parents do, we remembered our own youthful excursions and tests of independence. We not only fell into the "kids will be kids" stream of thought, we accentuated it with "boys will be boys." After all, we had grown out of those years of misguided non-maturity, and we were confident our kids would too. Of course, in the process of our waiting for him to "grow out of the need to experiment with alcohol," there were many instances of Michael being grounded, car keys taken away, and so forth.

On one such occasion, Michael's younger brother, Matt, was a big help!

One night when Michael came home, I noticed alcohol on his breath. The next morning I made him give me the keys to his pickup. Reluctantly, he did. Naturally, there was quite an argument. Seventeen year old boys don't just hand over their keys for a couple of weeks without words! Michael informed me that he would just drive the old beat up car that he had recently purchased to take to brandings. I told him I expected those keys also, when little brother Matt chimed in, "mom, you'll have to hide all the screwdrivers on the place if you want to keep him from driving his car." It was then I found out that there were no keys to the car, and it could only be started by using a screwdriver. Needless to say, the screwdrivers were also confiscated that day!

So, there we were – grounding and scolding, forcing him to face the consequences of underage drinking – or so we thought.

Little did we really realize just what consequences we would all face one day.

During Thanksgiving break of Michael's junior year, some of the college kids were home and one of them hosted a huge party at his house while his parents were visiting family out of town. A friend of Michael's was driving his pickup, and was involved in a minor accident on a gravel road. We got the call around midnight, when the sheriff's office told us Michael's pickup was in the process of being towed, and asked if we knew where Michael was. We didn't.

When the sheriff told us the kids were suspected of being at a party nearby the scene of the accident, we immediately went there, looking for him. We found him, literally hiding in the house.

We took him with us and went to the jail where we met the sheriff. He started interviewing Michael about the night's activities, and how the accident happened. Then the sheriff received a call about a major incident demanding his immediate attention. He told us just to take Michael home and he'd continue the conversation with him the next day.

Michael was furious with us for taking him to the jail to meet with the sheriff. He thought we were essentially turning him in, and thought that was a lousy thing for parents to do. We tried to explain that he needed to be punished for drinking, and even if he was not the one driving, his vehicle had been involved in an accident and he had to also accept some responsibility for that.

We did end up meeting with the sheriff the next day, where he officially gave Michael a ticket for Minor In Consumption. He had to go to court, where he was given a fine and required to take an alcohol evaluation exam within a few weeks.

We were okay with the punishment given by the court, although Michael wasn't, of course. It didn't help when he told us that an adult friend of ours had advised him that he could easily get out of any court punishment by telling the judge that the sheriff had no proof he had been drinking, because he failed to give him an official breath test or draw blood. We told Michael none of that mattered, because we knew he had been drinking, and so did the sheriff. The only reason the breath test was not given that night, was because of the emergency the sheriff was called to. Boy, did we ever get the cold shoulder from him for a few days – as we did from many of his friends, and even some other parents who thought we were wrong to allow the court to punish him with no physical evidence!

It's hard having your kids say and act like they literally hate you.

I've always believed that you should pick your battles with your kids. There were definitely times when we faltered in our discipline during Michael's senior year of high school. Roger and I actually battled more than either of us did with Michael himself. Roger and I were having a hard time agreeing on the way Michael should be disciplined. I think I tried to be forceful, wanting to treat Michael as a child, and Roger was trying to give him some room to grow and become independent.

I remember, very vividly now, one specific night that fateful spring of 2006, when I informed Roger that I wanted him to stand up with me and be stricter with Michael. I told him that I was not going to end up visiting Michael in jail some day if his partying and drinking hurt someone else, nor would I go to his funeral if he hurt himself. Roger told me to just back off of him for a while, before I made him want to leave the ranch and my nagging, and never return.

Looking back, that will probably go down as the second worse night and conversation in our entire marriage. Words spoken, can never be taken back. And no amount of "I'm sorry's" can compensate for some of those words spoken. And, sometimes, "I told you so" can become the most hurtful words one spouse can ever say to another.

The worst night's conversation between us happened just a few weeks after Michael died, when I spoke with venom, those very words, "I told you so."

Going back to the Thanksgiving weekend party of Michael's

junior year. The school's training rules policy toward alcohol use is this for athletes: the first time you get caught, you have to sit out the next event (game) you are in; the second time, it's two events; a third time and you are banned from participating. Since Michael only participated in football, and the policy carries forward from year to year, Michael was destined to sit on the bench for the first game of his senior year of football.

Michael was hoping the school would forget by the time football season rolled around, but of course they didn't. So, he sat on the bench that first game.

Knowing how much he loved to play football, and looked forward to playing that one year with his brother, who was a freshman, we were confident he had learned his lesson.

But the very next week, the school called us and said they had received an anonymous tip that Michael and a friend of his had been at a party the previous weekend, where alcohol was being served. When confronted, Michael admitted that yes, he had been there. However, he added that he did not drink, and left the scene of the party early. Even though there were numerous other students who came forward and agreed that Michael had not been drinking at that particular party, the school's stance was that he was at a party, in the presence of alcohol, and did not immediately leave, therefore once again breaking training rules.

I remember Michael telling us that he finally did not drink at a party, and he still was the one who was reprimanded, just for being there. I remember him saying that if he knew he was going to get into trouble anyway, he might as well have drank with the rest of the kids (of which only two others were similarly reprimanded).

It made me very angry, and also very sad, that this was the lesson Michael was learning.

We actually went as far as talking to a lawyer to defend Michael against the school's "anonymous tip," trying to lessen his punishment. When we found that it had been a teacher who had made the tip, based on student's conversations he had overheard, Michael told us just to let it go. He knew it would be a "he said – he said" kind of thing, and that he would end up losing. So we did.

Finally, halfway through the season, Michael was finally allowed to suit up and play. It was against the school's biggest rival. Michael caught a couple of wonderful touchdown receptions, and although the White River Tigers lost, which devastated him, I think he was really glad to be back on track with the team.

The next week they played in Philip, without Michael. But this time it was completely his choice. Throughout that summer and early fall, he had been riding bulls in the Northern Bull Riding tour. Amazingly, for his age, he qualified for the finals, which were held the last weekend in September in Sioux Falls. Bull riding always trumped any other activity Michael was involved in, even football.

Our family's plan was for Michael to go to Sioux Falls and ride in the first go-round Friday night, while Roger and I would go to Philip and watch Matt play football. Then we would go to Sioux Falls on Saturday, where we hoped Michael would be riding in the finals.

Friday night, just as we were leaving Philip, Michael called us and said he had ridden really well, and had qualified to ride on Saturday. He was ecstatic! But, he admitted that he had gotten stepped on, and his knee was kind of sore. He didn't sound overly worried or hurt, so we made plans to head east the next morning.

But the next morning, our daughter Amber, who lived in Sioux Falls, called to tell us that Michael had stayed at her house the night before, and that he was very sick. She said she was going to take him to the emergency room and have his knee checked out because he couldn't even stand on it. A little while later she called and said that the doctor gave Michael some pain medicine, and said he was ok to ride, as long as he felt ok.

We decided to not go to Sioux Falls then, because we were sure that even if he was feeling well enough to ride, he wouldn't do well. He was there with a friend, and we weren't worried about him getting home, since the friend would be able to drive. As we suspected, Michael was not even able to get on a bull in the chutes – he was in too much pain.

The next morning, he and his friend headed for home. Since

they had borrowed our car, and the friend lived in Winner, Roger and I went to Winner to meet the boys so Michael wouldn't have to drive the rest of the way home by himself. What we saw shocked us. Michael had a very high fever, chills, and had been vomiting most of the way back. We took him straight to the hospital in Pierre.

At first, the doctors were fearful of meningitis because of his symptoms. They performed a spinal tap, which was nearly as painful for me to watch, as it was for him to receive. Fortunately, those results were negative. But he did have damage in his knee from being stepped on Friday night. He was scheduled for surgery the next morning to remove a portion of torn meniscus lining. The surgery went well, but he developed an infection. Because they couldn't get it controlled, he ended up staying in the hospital for a full week.

When we finally brought him home, he very solemnly told me, "You know, I wish I would have just gone to the football game."

He was on crutches and in and out of school for a few weeks then. The secretary at his school jokingly told him that he should write a book about his senior year, as it was starting out with a lot of adventure and drama. By the time deer season rolled around in November, Michael was doing well, and once again, back on track.

The next few weeks were pretty uneventful, as he spent most of his time lifting weights and training to get his strength back for the upcoming late winter rodeo season.

He had qualified to ride at the 20X Extreme High School rodeo performance at the Black Hills Stock Show. I had purchased four front row tickets to the PBR Bull Riding, which was held the night before the high school rodeo. Naturally, mother nature didn't cooperate, and we weren't able to leave the ranch that day. Since we couldn't get away for the whole weekend, I gave the tickets to Michael and his friends. He was so happy, and called home that night to tell us how exciting it was to be there in person.

The next day, right as we were leaving to go to Rapid City and watch him, he called home. I answered the phone, and he sheepishly said, "Mom, could you guys come up here a little early? I need you to bail me out of jail."

I was absolutely furious! I told him that if this was how he was going to thank us for allowing him to spend the weekend there with his friends, by drinking and getting thrown in jail – on the eve of a very important and prestigious rodeo, and that if going out and drinking was more important than preparing for riding, then he could just spend the whole day in jail. I was absolutely serious. Like I said, I was furious!

At some point, during my ranting and raving to him on the phone, I began to hear him chuckle. Then I heard laughing in the background. And finally, he began roaring with laughter. It had all been a joke. He was very good at "pushing my buttons" and getting me all worked up and worried. And it definitely worked that day! He and his friends got a good laugh at my expense. So I calmed down, and we headed to the rodeo.

Shortly after that, Michael entered a rodeo in Nebraska. Once again, we got a call from him saying he had been stepped on; this time it was his foot. Thankfully, although it did break a small bone near his heel, it didn't require hospitalization. He was advised to wear a boot-brace for a few weeks. Again, the crutches were used.

When he went back to school a couple of days later, the secretary just smiled, and told him to get to work on his book!

The next chapter of Michael's story that year happened on the eve of Palm Sunday. Saturday afternoon, he decided to go to town and pick up some friends to spend the day with. He took a .22 rifle and his rod and reel, because he wasn't sure if they would end up shooting prairie dogs, or fishing. It wasn't unusual for Michael to come home between midnight and 1:00 a.m. on a Sunday morning, after being out Saturday night, so we weren't expecting him to drive up at 8:00 p.m. that night. Not only was he home early, but he was in bed very shortly after, without hardly saying a word to us other than that they had been shooting prairie dogs. I was pretty sure that he must have been getting sick.

The next morning I began the task of cleaning out our garage, and had the boys bring a pick-up to the house to load up the junk to haul to our dump. I noticed that when Michael walked, he had a very slight limp, but hardly gave it a second thought.

While the boys were gone, I got a phone call from a friend who had been hunting with Michael the previous day, asking if he was ok. Not having a clue what he was talking about, I told him if he knew something he thought a mother should know, he had better "fess up" quick.

Apparently, while shooting prairie dogs, the friends' gun fired when it shouldn't have, and the bullet hit the ground just a few feet from where Michael was standing. Pieces of the bullet ricocheted on impact with the rocks, and some fragments found their way to Michael's leg.

When he pulled into the driveway, he knew right away that I had found out. I made him show me the wound. It really didn't look bad. There was a pin-point mark on his knee (his good knee) where a piece of metal was embedded, and another one in his thigh.

He had plans to ride some practice bulls that afternoon, and he said he was just going to stop at the Winner Hospital on his way and have them take the pieces of shrapnel out. I couldn't believe his naivety in the matter! I kind of freaked out a little, and tried to explain the seriousness of the situation, even if it didn't look that bad! I told him that whenever a shooting accident happens, no matter how accidental it was (and I knew this was very accidental), the doctors would have to report it to law enforcement officials. So then – he asked me if I could just "dig out" the metal with a needle and tweezers! He didn't want his friend to get into any trouble.

After a short, but loud, "no I will absolutely not do that!" from me, we headed to the Pierre hospital to have it looked at.

Once at the hospital, everything happened pretty much as expected. They did have to call the local sheriff, and Michael had to make a statement. It was pretty simple, and no charges were ever filed. But, it had to be reported.

As for the shrapnel in his knee and thigh – the doctor decided the piece in his knee should be removed. It was lodged near the joint, and if not removed, they thought that someday it might move and then cause another round of problems. As for the piece in his thigh – it was embedded in muscle. It was such a small piece that the doctor said it would do more damage to try to remove it, than to just let it go. He said Michael would never know it was there.

Surgery that afternoon didn't last very long, nor did the recovery. By midnight they had released Michael to go home. Once out of town, he looked over and very solemnly said, "I sure wish we would have gone fishing yesterday." It was becoming common for him to "wish" he had chosen a different activity! The next day, it was back to normal – Michael on crutches for a few days!

During the previous few months, Michael and I had argued to the point that we just quit talking about it - where to get his senior pictures taken. He wanted to go to a professional photographer, and I wanted to take the pictures myself. We had a very nice camera at my job, and the company I worked for does professional photo printing, so I could save a lot of money by taking them myself. I know Michael thought they would turn out bad, and it just wouldn't be cool to have your mom take your senior photos.

Finally, on April 15, I won the long standing argument. With graduation just a month away, we were really pushing to get pictures taken and printed, and announcements made and sent. Later that afternoon I told Roger and Michael that I was taking his photos that day, and that was the end of it. Michael changed into some good clothes, grabbed his bull vest and chaps – I grabbed a couple more of his shirts, and we all drove down to our corrals.

On the way, I had Michael stand by some yucca plants for a photo; we had him pose near a fence; we made sure there were cattle in the background of some photos; in general, we all had a fun time. An hour later we were downloading the photos onto the computer. I think Michael was even a little bit impressed with the outcome. Of course, Michael was so very photogenic, it was very, very easy.

The month of May began as normal as ever. There was a high school practice rodeo in Kadoka the first Friday, where Roger went with Michael and unfortunately, watched him buck off. The next day was White River's high school rodeo. I was there taking lots of photos of him and other local kids, but as the day before, he bucked off.

Sunday's rodeo was in Burke. Roger took Michael, and I really considered going along, but at the last minute I decided to stay home and do some housework. My justification was that we would be having company for graduation in a couple of weeks, and since I was at the rodeo all day Saturday I was kind of behind in doing laundry and cleaning. Plus, I remember saying, "There will be lots of rodeos all summer. It won't hurt for me just to miss this next one."

So Roger and Mikey went to Burke, and it turned out to be a very good thing that at least Roger was with him. He rode his bull that day. It was the last rodeo he ever went to, the last time his dad ever saw him doing what he loved, and doing it well.

Brandings consumed the next days leading up to graduation. Every afternoon after school, and all day after the senior's last day, Michael was earning money for his summer rodeo entries. He had such big plans for the summer. He was expecting to go to the high school finals, riding in the Northern Bull Riding tour again, some 4-H rodeos, and hoping to enter a number of SDRA rodeos.

Saturday night, May 13, we had a family get together to celebrate his upcoming graduation the next day. Sunday, he left before noon to go pick up a fellow classmate before the big ceremony. Half an hour before it was to begin, I was waiting to line the whole class up for one last photo for the newspaper - but no Michael and friend. They were nearly late, and I was just "beyond words" mad. Neither was answering their phones. For some reason, it never occurred to me to be concerned about their safety. I just thought they had been messing around and forgot about the time. When they finally strolled into the gym, I met them at the door and instantly started chewing both out for almost being late and embarrassing their whole class.

What I didn't know until later, was that nearly the whole class knew why they were late. Apparently, they had driven to another town to pick up some more alcohol for the graduation party they were planning that night.

During the graduation ceremony, there was a time when each of the students presented their parents with a flower. Michael gave one to each of his grandmothers, then brought one to me. We hugged, and I whispered in his ear that even though I had been mad at him for almost being late, I loved him and was proud of him. He said, "I know, mom."

After the formal ceremony, everyone moved to the old gym for the kids' receptions. Once again, I was behind the camera lens, snapping photo after photo of Michael and the rest of our family. When I asked him to round up his three closest friends for a group picture in their caps and gowns, Michael told me they had already changed because it was so hot in the added clothing. I told Roger that before they all left for college the next fall, I was going to have to get them together for a "cap and gown" photo. Who knew – that would never be possible in just a few hours.

We went then, to Roger's parents house, to relax and have kind of a "family only" reception for Michael. It was there that he told us about the party the class had planned. Roger and his brother started reminiscing about their own graduation party – where it was held, how long it lasted, and how much fun they had. That's when Michael told us they had been picking up some of the alcohol earlier that day. He didn't say who had bought it for them, and we didn't ask. I suppose we thought - he's 18 years old and he just graduated from high school – let him grow up, and let him enjoy it.

Roger had been planning to move cattle to a different pasture the next morning, in preparation for branding later that week. Before he left Sunday evening, Michael asked what time Roger wanted to get started, so he'd be home to help. Roger told him that he'd changed his mind, and would wait until Monday afternoon or evening to move the cattle. He told Michael that the important thing, since we knew he'd be drinking all night, was to just stay where the party was and to sleep it off before coming home. He told Michael to either stay at the party sight, or stay at a friend's house nearby, but to make sure he didn't drive home.

Of course, like most red-blooded American teenage boys, those words were music to Michael's ears. He had just been given permission to stay out all night long! He agreed to not drive home until he was sober. I will never forget his words, as he strolled down the driveway to his car. He looked back and said, "ok mom, see you tomorrow afternoon." He was smiling from ear to ear.

It was such a relief to get home that night. We piled his cards and gifts on a chair, and heaved great sighs. Michael made it through high school. He would be going off to college in the fall. His life as an adult was beginning! I think it's at that point of high school graduation, as a parent, that I thought – I did ok with him. He's a good person, and I've taught him well. He'll be ok. Sleep that night, came very easy.

Just as we became confident that Michael's life as an adult was beginning, in reality, his life was ending. Just before 8 a.m. the next morning, May 15, 2006, our lives, too, started to end.

Chapter 1

Monday, May 15, 2006

It is Monday night, and Michael is stable. He did not have surgery today, but they did drain the blood and fluid from his lungs. Thankfully, he is not bleeding into his lungs, and they think what was there was caused by bleeding from a broken nose.

Michael does not have any broken bones that they know of right now. There may be some in his face, but they're not very concerned about that as of now. His spleen has a tear in it, but they are hopeful it will heal itself. If it does start to bleed, they will go in right away and remove it. So far, things look positive.

They will be doing another CT tomorrow morning. His brain was without oxygen, but for how long, they're not sure. By continuing to do CTs periodically, they will be seeing if there is any brain damage.

He is on a ventilator, which is breathing for him. They are doing this so his body doesn't have to do that work, and can put more energy into healing. Hopefully, sometime tomorrow they will start to take him off the ventilator.

They have kept Michael sedated all day today.

We truly appreciate everyone's phone calls and prayers. Please continue. I know the prayers are being answered.

When we're in the room with him we have to turn our phones off, so if we don't answer your call, that's where we're at. We'll update this site every few hours, so you can always check here also.

Thanks for your concerns, caring, and above all, your prayers.

Tuesday, May 16, 2006 8:55 a.m.

It's Tuesday morning and Michael is still stable. Yesterday they drained the blood and fluid from his lungs, and they're planning to drain some more this morning. They are currently doing CT scans of his brain and abdomen area. They say it's a waiting game now, to see if there is any brain damage that might not be showing up on the CT scan. They took him off the ventilator last night, and it took him 2 1/2 minutes to start breathing on his own, so they put him back on the ventilator. They no longer have him sedated with medicine, but he is still in a coma. His vital signs are good this morning and his heart rate has gone down to around 95-100. It was around 130 yesterday. They said one of the reasons it has been so high is because it was bruised during the impact, similar to that of having had a heart attack. His lungs were also badly bruised. They are expecting him to develop pneumonia, and are starting him on antibiotics also.

Other than that, we don't know much. We're just staying with him, and talking to him. We're telling him, constantly, when we're able to be with him, your messages and well wishes. We truly believe he hears us, and is grateful, as are we, for all of your caring and support.

Keep those prayers going. We know it works!!!

We'll update again this afternoon.

Tuesday, May 16, 2006 11:32 a.m.

It's about noon on Tuesday. I didn't expect to update this so soon, but we just got some more information about Michael from the CT scan he had this morning.

First - the good news - they drained his lungs again, and they look good now.

But it seems that Michael has some serious brain damage. The doctor said that it could be as though he has had a stroke. They just took him back for another scan and possibly an angiogram of the brain? I'm not really sure what they called it. But they did it in a hurry. They hope this test will help show them the severity of the damage. They said that he should be awake by now, and since he isn't, they've become very concerned.

Roger and I read the guest book messages, and I will relay them to Michael the minute they let us see him again! We cried when we read them. They are so thoughtful, and we are so appreciative of all your support.

Please keep praying as this latest news is very worrisome.

Tuesday, May 16, 2006 2:01 p.m.

Many of you have already heard, but for those of you who haven't, things have taken a bad turn for Michael. A neurosurgeon has checked him and has bad news. He said that Michael was without oxygen long enough that he has severe brain damage. They have done three catscans and each shows progressivly more damage. They will not do another until tomorrow. He said that this injury will be what takes Michael's life.

We believe, and will continue to believe, that they are wrong. We know how incredibly tough and stubborn Mikey is. Please, please don't stop praying. I have been telling God that he doesn't need anymore good kids with him right now. Please keep this continuing.

Thanks you all for your caring and love.

Tuesday, May 16, 2006 7:48 p.m.

Thank you everyone, for the absolutely warm and caring thoughts and prayers you have shared with us. We are so moved by the prayer service held for Michael. We had one here in the Chapel of the hospital at the same time.

We will continue to give Michael as much time as he needs to heal. We have also turned Michael's care over to God. We know that whatever happens will be God's will and not ours. And God knows best about what Michael needs. God has given us the miracle of Michael, and whether God chooses to let him live with us, or takes him home to live with Him, either will be a miracle. Spending eternity in Heaven with our Father has to be a miracle in itself. Of course we are still praying that God's will is the same as ours.

Thank you - all of you - for all of your caring. It is incredible, and we are printing and reading all of your messages to Michael. We know he thanks all of you too.

Wednesday, May 17, 2006 9:34 a.m.

Well, another day, and Michael is still with us. I'm sorry it has been so many hours since we checked in here. It was a long night, with little sleep.

Things are much the same today. Right now Michael's heart rate is very high and his temperature is a little high. They say that's because his body is no longer able to regulate it's temperature. The medication they gave him yesterday to help drain the fluid from his brain - well, they gave him as much as they could, and it hasn't worked. His body is beginning to dehydrate, so they're actually giving him fluids now. It doesn't seem to make sense, but then what does right now.

A couple of doctors have seen him this morning, but the neurosurgeon hasn't. Since there has virtually been no change, they're not expecting the neuro to order a catscan test today. But we should know more regarding that in the next hour or so.

The responses from all of you is incredible. I can't imagine someone we haven't heard from or who hasn't been here. It is very reassuring to know that Michael is so loved by not only us, but all of you. Thank you again, and please continue to pray for our Mikey.

Wednesday, May 17, 2006 11:19 a.m.

We are very hopeful right now. More so than we've been in the last 24 hours. Michael moved twice during the hourly neuro test at 10 a.m. At 11 a.m. he moved three times. Just a couple of minutes ago the nurse checked his temperature - put the thing in his ear - and he moved his head! His temp is down to 97.8 from over 99 earlier today.

But his heart rate is very high, as is his blood pressure, so they kicked us all out for a few minutes to let him calm down.

We are all so excited, and the atmosphere here in the waiting room is just incredible. While we're in the room with Michael, the girls out here are going to keep you all posted, so you might be hearing from a lot more people than just me for a while.

It is working - the prayers are working!!!! THANK YOU ALL FROM THE BOTTOM OF OUR HEARTS!!!

Wednesday, May 17, 2006 3:21 p.m.

I don't exactly know how to do this. But at 2:36 this afternoon Michael passed away. I'll explain more later.

Thank you for all your prayers, and please continue praying. We trust in the Lord Jesus Christ that His will was done. We are comforted by that.

Wednesday, May 17, 2006 5:30 p.m.

Just a note to let you all know we really appreciate all of your messages and thoughts for us now.

Roger and I just finished visiting with Life Source, the organization that handles organ donations. We know that Michael was always willing to give anything he had to someone who might need something. This is why we decided to have his organs donated. We know this is what Michael would have wanted.

Thursday, May 18, 2006

First of all, I would like to thank everyone for all of the support and prayers in the past few days. It has really helped us to read your caring words and know that there are so many people who loved Mikey and care so much about our family. I am so grateful to all of you; you don't know what a blessing you have been to us.

I never thought I would lose a little brother - it never crossed my mind. I think my entire family is numb right now – we don't know what life is like without him and never wanted to find out. I wanted to write to all of you and let you know how much we all appreciate everything you have done for us, but I'm not sure what the right words are right now.

Thank you so much to all of Mike's friends who were there this week to support us and talk to Mike. I know he heard us and he went to Heaven knowing how much each and every one of us loves him. I'm grateful that we all were able to talk to him before he left us. He's in a better place now and it's comforting to know this.

We never knew my Uncle Cliff, but I'm sure he's taking Mike to all of the great rodeos in heaven! I bet they're having a blast

27

together. Mike always loved the movie 8 Seconds and when we were kids we probably watched that movie a million times over and over – Lane Frost was Mikey's hero and now he finally gets to meet him! Mike was a great cowboy and a great person – he had the biggest heart I've ever seen. Katelyn loved her Uncle Mikey so much and it breaks my heart that he won't be around to help her grow up, but I asked him to watch over her and be her guardian angel and I know he will do that. She was the only one in our family that he let drive his new car!!

I know Mike is looking down on all of us and knowing how much we miss him being here, but we will be with him again someday and I know he will watch over us all until then.

Amber

Thursday, May 18, 2006

Roger, Matt and I are back home now, Thursday evening. I am in awe over the number of people who are concerned for our family right now. We stopped in Chamberlain on our way home today to get Matt a suit for the funeral, and everyone at Ray's knew of Michael's passing - because they all knew him and loved him. The friends he made covered the four corners of the state, and beyond.

We have been sharing wonderful memories of Michael today, almost like he's here with us.

My prayer now is that none of you parents ever have to face such sadness and loss, and for those of you who have - my heart aches for you even more now, now that I do know what you endured.

By now, Michael's organs are in the process of saving other's lives, giving great joy and hope to parents who may have been facing their worst nightmare. It comforts us to know that.

We will be meeting with the funeral home tomorrow, and will let all of you know, also through here, of the arrangements.

And, lastly, thank you to everyone who came out today and got our calves branded! And to everyone at the papers who worked so much harder this week - thanks from the bottom of my heart.

28

Friday, May 19, 2006

It is Friday evening, and has been a very trying day. We made Michael's funeral arrangements today. The funeral will be Monday at 2:00 p.m. CST at the school's Community Events Center in White River. There will also be a viewing available at Sandoz Chapel of the Pines in Valentine, Nebr. on Sunday from 4-9 p.m.

Right before we left today, we got the most incredible phone call. Life Source called to let us know that Michael's organs were all viable - and through their recipients surgeries, saved eight lives last night.

Michael's heart went to a 41 year old father, who was minutes away from dying when Michael's heart arrived for him - in Minnesota. Both lungs were ok - one went to a 58 year old woman and the other to a 53 year old man - both in Minnesota. Onw kidney went to a 29 year old right at McKennan Hospital in Sioux Falls, and the other to a 34 year old recipient. His pancreas went to a 32 year old female. And his liver was able to be divided with half going to a 10-month old baby and the other half going to someone in Chicago, Illinois.

They said that eight life-saving organs is the most that anyone would be able to give, and is very rare. But Mikey did it. Just another testament to the kind of kid he was!

Even though planning our child's funeral was the saddest thing I've ever had to do, it really made us feel better knowing what had just happened. On our way to the funeral home we were very quiet and Roger said, "Can you imagine how those eight families are feeling today?" I think I could. It's how I would be feeling if somehow Michael were alive and well at home right now.

Last night I got the most sleep I've had at one time since this nightmare began. I went into his bedroom to just smell him. I cuddled up with his blankets and clothes on his bed, and fell asleep for a whole three hours! It was wonderful. When he was a baby he would never take an afternoon nap unless I was laying beside him with my arms around him. I think now the only way I can sleep is if his arms, even if through his blankets, are around me.

Thank you for all of your constant care for our family!

Sunday, May 21, 2006

I let the journal entry lapse yesterday. I found that it was a day that I just couldn't deal with much. I needed to be alone, so I went to Pierre. I think I'm most alone in a city surrounded by people. Roger and Matt said the house was full all afternoon with visitors, and I am sorry I missed most of you. There were a bunch of kids here when I got home, and that was nice. I've always felt good when the house was full of the kids' friends.

This afternoon we go to Valentine once again for the viewing of Michael's body. It will be the first time seeing him since Wednesday night when we said goodbye. I think God sent the clouds today to match our mood.

I heard that the school counselor is going to meet with Michael's classmates tonight, to prepare them for the funeral tomorrow. What a thoughtful thing to do. We're very grateful for everyone's compassion toward his friends, who are just more of "our kids".

I would like to share one very special memory of Michael with all of you, and also invite you to share yours with us through here. We're going to make a remembrance book of Michael, and welcome all of yours.

A couple of years ago we were at a Little Britches rodeo at the Seven Down arena in Spearfish, in January (indoor arena). The weather became horrible on Sunday, and of course bull riding is the last event of the day. In the order of events, Sr. Boys Bulls were followed by Jr. Boys Bulls, which ended the rodeo. I told Michael that the minute he was done riding I wanted to head for home because I knew it would be a very long drive on very bad roads, and didn't want the interstate to close and get us stuck in Spearfish another day. He agreed. But - he was the last of the Sr. Boys to ride, naturally. I still thought he would be finding me shortly. (In Little Britches, parents are not allowed behind the chutes). But he didn't come, and didn't come, and didn't come. And I just couldn't see him from where I was. I even had someone have the announcer announce for him to go the the front door. But he still didn't come. They had begun to buck the Jr. Bullriders.

Pretty soon they were just about finished, and I was steaming mad. I thought we had wasted about an hour and was ready to chew his butt when I found him.

Finally - he came strolling down the alleyway and was I ready to lay into him. But a man and a little, maybe 10 year old boy, came up to him in front of me. The man reached out and shook Michael's hand and thanked him profusely. The little boy had a grin from ear to ear! Apparently, it was the little boy's first rodeo, and he got very scared when it came time to get on his bull. Michael stayed behind the chute (since his dad couldn't) and helped calm him down, and showed him what to do. The boy ended up winning first place.

When I heard this I almost cried. We walked out of the arena and I was very quiet. We made it home without a problem, although quite late. And I was never so proud of my son. Michael had a wild side, but at the end of the day, this is the kind of person he was!

Rejoicing in all of God's blessings.

Monday, May 22, 2006

It is Monday, May 22, 2006, the day we will ceremonially say goodbye to Michael and commit his body back to the earth. Today we will celebrate Michael's life. Michael celebrated his life every day.

It is exactly one week since his accident. It seems like the week has flown by, and it also seems like the week has moved in slow motion. At times I think I can remember every second that has passed these last seven days.

As I write this and gaze out the window, the weather looks beautiful. The sky is bright and clear. There is a breeze right now, and Roger said the wind is supposed to pick up. I think the wind is perfect for today. It will lift up our spirits and help send our thoughts and prayers to Heaven.

I pray for all of our and Michael's friends and family to feel the presence of our Lord Jesus Christ on this special day!

Tuesday, May 23, 2006

Well, we made it through yesterday. People are saying that things will never get better, but they will get easier. They are so right. Every day now, is a day to celebrate all we have. We miss Michael incredibly, and can't imagine life without him, but Amber and Matt and all of their and Michael's friends are who we have to live for now; and our gorgeous granddaughter Katelyn, who has been a welcome distraction from our sadness the past few days.

I am still in awe over the e-mails and comments posted to this sight daily. I know I've said it before, but it seems I can't say it enough - the support we've been getting is just overwhelming.

The funeral service yesterday was beautiful. We've had a lot of people thank us for allowing Michael's organs to be donated. And we've been saying all along that some good absolutely has to come from Michael's death. The life giving organs was a good thing, and it has been called a "gift of life." But I think that the message at the service yesterday was better.

The gym was the fullest I have ever seen it - hundreds and hundreds of friends came to honor Michael. And these hundreds of people, through the inspiring message from Pastor Jackie, were given the opportunity right there to choose to be saved. Michael's death brought those people there, to hear the message - possibly having never heard it before. I prayed that everyone's heart was open to her words. I pray that everyone touched by Michael will someday spend eternity in Heaven with him and God, through the "gift of life" given by Jesus Christ. This will be the best thing to come from Michael's death.

As for the organ donation process - many have asked me to explain just how it works. It too has brought us great comfort, and I will provide the specific information in our circumstance later today, through this journal.

We are truly blessed to have the friends we do, as was Michael.

Tuesday, May 23, 2006

It's starting to get late, and I realized I said I would update the journal about organ donations. So, here goes -

When Michael moved some on Wednesday morning, and our initial reaction was that things were looking up, we found out that it was really the beginning of the end of his life. The movements were actually caused because his brain was starting to hemorrhage. They told us the day before that when this happened, he wouldn't have much time left at all. We just weren't aware of the signs. His heart rate going up was another sign. The doctor and nurses of course knew what was happening, but were very considerate of our feelings, and let us have that short moment of hope. When it finally dawned on Roger and I what was really happening, we became selfish and asked the rest of our family and all of his friends to just wait in the waiting room. We spent the last three hours completely alone with Michael. They scheduled a series of tests for 2:30 that afternoon, which would affirm that Michael was brain-dead.

They told us at around 11:00 that he was still breathing very slightly on his own. The ventilator was set at a number 8, and he was getting 11 (not exactly sure what those numbers signify), which meant some of his air was coming in by his own means. They said when both numbers on the machine showed 8, it would mean that he was no longer breathing for himself - the final sign. At 12:15, and I'll never forget it - after praying, I talked to Mikey. I told him that it was okay for him to leave me, because God was waiting for him, and he didn't have to keep struggling and trying for me.

At 12:35 he quit breathing at all on his own, and I knew in my heart that he had gone. But we waited, and I held his hand until the scheduled time for the tests, which were positive. The doctor pronounced the time of death at 2:36 p.m. I will probably always feel a sense of guilt for telling Mikey he could go. Right now, writing this, my heart is racing and I can hardly see for the tears. I pray every day that it was the right thing to say to him. It was excruciating to let Michael go.

We had told the nurse in those two hours that we would like to talk to someone about organ donations. She told us that they also wanted to talk to us, but wanted to wait until the time was right.

They were so considerate and compassionate to us - it made the conversation very easy, considering.

We were told that if we chose to do this, Michael's organs would be kept working until all the pieces were in place - matches would have to be found and each respective doctor would have to be flown in to Sioux Falls to retrieve each organ and take it back to where the recipient would be. They said it could take up to 24 hours to get things ready. She also told us that when we went to see Michael again, he wouldn't look any different to us, and the care they would give him would be no less. That was true. They still turned his body every two hours, and I watched them caringly comb his hair. He was treated with the utmost respect and care.

We were told of each organ we could donate, and each one had to be given it's own permission. We said yes to each vital organ. They said they wouldn't know until they began the surgical procedure if any of the organs would still be viable though. They asked a lot of questions about Michael - his likes and his personality. We shared many memories of him with them.

We went back to Michael after all the organ donor paperwork was finished. He was in the same room as before, and we said what we thought was our final goodbyes to him.

Then we allowed the rest of our family and all of the kids there to go in and say their goodbyes. There was a nurse with us in the waiting room when we told everyone of Michael's passing. She helped explain what they would expect when seeing him again - that he would look the same, and the machines would still be hooked up, as they had to be to keep the organs working, but that he was gone.

When everyone had left the hospital, Roger, Matt, Amber and I stayed behind to collect our thoughts. Before we left that night, I just had to go in and say goodbye again - this time for the final time. The nurse said we could stay as long as we wanted. She said that some people even stay with a loved one until they are taken to surgery for the organ retrieval. We chose not to do this. It wasn't going to happen until Thursday sometime, and we knew that Michael was gone. The procedure took place Thursday afternoon, and eight surgeries followed Thursday evening. Eight families celebrated life on Friday morning.

Wednesday, May 24, 2006

Today was not a very good day.

Michael has been gone for a few days before, and that's what it kind of feels like. But today, I thought he should be coming home. He's been gone long enough.

Usually, when he came home, he would leave his gear bag in the middle of the office floor and his boots in the middle of the entryway floor. Then he'd take a shower and there would be wet towels all over the bathroom floor. He'd toss some clothes into the washing machine and pretty soon I'd have a mix of wet, semi-wet and dry clothes all over the laundry room floor. And as soon as this mess was started, he'd have his feet propped up and the tv set to the PBR. I'd start complaining about what a mess he made, and go around picking things up. And of course, his phone would be ringing off the hook - reliving the weekend bullriding, or planning to go to an upcoming branding.

I'd be asking if he had his schoolwork done, and was he ready for semester tests. He would assure me he had. I would know that he hadn't. Instead, we'd talk about his last bullriding, and the next one coming up. We'd talk about his checking account, and make sure he was keeping it balanced. He'd assure me he had. I would know that he hadn't. He would know that I knew, and would raise one eyebrow slyly. He'd tell a couple of jokes and laugh at me when I didn't get them.

Then we'd plan the next day – what he and Matt had to do after school, when everyone was expected home, who would drive to town. We would all go to bed about the same time. But he would get up half an hour later or so and go back to finish watching some more bullriding on tv. He didn't think I knew. But I knew.

Instead, today, I opened up a Michael Glynn Memorial Fund savings account at the bank for the memorial gifts people have been sending in his honor.

It was hard to be around people in town, who were going

about their regular routines. I have to rebuild my regular routine, to one that does not include Michael's schedule. Then I went to the cemetery and visited his gravesite for the first time since the funeral. The wind was blowing ferociously and the flowers were drying out badly. It looked sad.

I finished the day by reading his obituary in some of the papers.

Today was not a very good day.

Thursday, May 25, 2006

By the time I got home today I thought that if one more person hugged me I would choke them! My emotions have been one huge roller coaster ride that past few days! I don't want anyone to check on me and make sure I'm ok!

I used to jump the fence if he didn't get out of the arena right away, or if he got hung up, and it embarrassed Michael so much! I did that once at the Yellow Rose in Platte and he wouldn't talk to me all the way home. And he was only about 12 years old.

Well, I eventually grew out of that stage. It was at the bull-riding in White River, and he got kicked by the bull. He got out of the arena, but they were putting a bandage on his leg behind the chutes, and you could see them from the grandstand. A friend asked me how I could stand to not go back there with him. Believe me - it took some doing, and a real desire to not embarrass him by making him look like a "mommy's boy" in front of the other guys.

It's kind of like the lyrics to a song that was played on the video at the funeral – "you're proud when they walk, scared when they run." Sometimes, now, I wish I had said no to everything he wanted to do. But then, I realize that would have killed his spirit.

I do wish I would have been much, much stronger and more vocal about drinking and driving.

We knew he had gone out drinking with his friends before, and I would sit on pins and needles until he got home. I have this feeling that he became as complacent about that behavior as we had. We of course told him it was wrong, and would punish him as appropriately as we thought we could, and pray that he wouldn't do it again. But I think that he thought he was invincible, as many teenagers do. Every time he was out and alcohol was involved, and he made it home, gave him confidence that he could handle it. Until the fateful morning when he didn't handle it.

Why do we worry so much about getting kicked by a bull, or falling off a horse? And we worry so little about kids drinking and driving? Maybe because a lot more of us drank and drove, than rode bulls, and we are here today, believing we handled it then and can handle it now. And since we handled it then, we too think our kids can handle it now. Many, many, many more kids (and adults) are killed or have their lives changed for the worse due to alcohol, than due to rodeo or sports injuries.

We have lost Mikey, and I can't get him back. But I can do my best to not lose anyone else I love.

I don't know how this is going to go over with our neighbors, and friends, but from this point on, there will be no alcohol at my house for branding crews, etc. If there are any kids or teenagers around, I will never have alcohol available for the adults. We've got to let kids know that they can have fun without alcohol. We've got to be better role models for them. It's just so sad that it takes something like Michael's death to wake me up.

But let me offer this to everyone out there - let me go through the pain of losing a child. Let me feel that emptiness and loneliness. Let me worry endlessly about my other children who have lost their sibling. All I ask in return is that you become more vocal, also, in your community, and try to put a stop to kids believing they are invincible. If this can happen to my child, it could happen to yours. Let me grieve now, so you don't have to yourself one day.

With God all things are possible!

Saturday, May 27, 2006

A few people have lately said they can't believe we haven't shown anger towards God for taking Michael from our lives. Why would I be angry with God? He gave us 18 years with Michael, not to mention our other children and all of the thousands of blessings we have every day – if we just take the time to see that they are blessings! Why should I be angry with God, when there are so many others out there I feel so justified in directing anger at right now? Take today, for example.

I got the mail, and was reading the lovely cards and messages our friends sent. Then I opened up a large envelope and inside found a laminated copy of Michael's obituary from a newspaper. There was a form letter from a company that sells headstones, telling me that "they are very sorry for my loss" and "when I'm ready" to call them about purchasing a headstone for my loved one's grave. They said their prices are very competitive, etc., etc., etc.

I find this behavior from a business to be rude and very distasteful. My son's funeral was only five days ago, and already this company is looking to profit from my loss. I realize that selling headstones is their business, and a business that is needed. But I think their timing is bad, to say the least, and their way of making me aware of their business is just as bad. Do they think that after a family has had to go through the process of planning a funeral, they can't figure out on their own that they will need a headstone for the grave? Why don't they just advertise in newspapers, and stay away from those tacky "you've just been approved a $10,000 line of credit" kind of junk mail letters. I think it's very inconsiderate for them to conduct business this way. Them sending a copy of the obituary reminded me of the so-called ambulance chaser lawyers. These guys must read the papers for the obituaries, then send the obituaries to families, trying to trap a new customer. I think it's disgusting.

They also sent a small package of rosemary, saying we should spread it over our loved one's grave because would make us feel better.

I threw it away. It stunk.

Sunday, May 28, 2006

Roger and Matt built a wooden cross for Michael's grave today, and I painted his name on the front of it. I bundled up all of the flowers from the funeral, and we headed to the cemetery. Digging a hole for the cross was definitely a labor of love on Roger's part, as the ground was almost rock-hard dry. But he planted the cross a good two feet into the ground, and it seems to be sturdy enough.

How our lives have changed. This Sunday afternoon we should have been holding our breath waiting for Mikey to come out of a chute at some rodeo.

It was good to go to town today. I'm taking baby steps, getting back to being a part of society. Each time I'm around people, it gets easier.

We had a good conversation with some friends at the cemetery today. We were talking about kids learning a lesson from Michael's accident. We were talking about the young people, and some not-so-young people, who buy the alcohol for minors. We were talking about how some parents get mad at the authorities when they get a phone call in the middle of the night, saying that their child has been stopped for a DUI or MIC or a similar incident, and they have to go pick them or their car up. What I wouldn't give tonight to get a call like that, so I could simply go to town and bring Michael home with me. I pray that those parents realize that the alternative to such a phone call could very easily be frequent visits to a cemetery to visit their child.

A similar conversation happened the other day. The question arose – what constitutes that a person a day short of their 21st birthday is too young and irresponsible to drink, and two days later, they are considered an adult and capable of drinking responsibly?

Roger and I have gone out for dinner before with our kids, and had a drink or two. One of us always drove home, and we thought we were fine. We were. But did our kids know that? Didn't they just see us drinking and driving? And didn't their young minds think that they could one day do the same thing? After all, they grow up mimicking the adults in their lives. We tell them, don't do this, then we do it ourselves, in front of them. I feel so sorry for my kids – the mixed messages we've been sending them – it's horrible! I know – we've always said "you can do certain things when you're an adult" or "when you're older". But kids have no patience. They look at a 30 year old person and call them a dinosaur. They can't wait to grow up and experiment all the things we've told them they have to wait for. So they choose to not wait.

I'm going to choose now to try to do my best to be a better role model for the people in my community. It's going to start in my home. I don't think I could go through losing another child of my own. I wouldn't wish this experience on my worst enemy.

I think when people try to do good deeds on their own - well, why? It takes so little to ask for God's help. And He's sitting there waiting to give it! With prayer, we can change society. With prayer, we can make a difference!

Monday, May 29, 2006

Today was beautiful, especially after the damaging hailstorm we had last night. As Matt and I sat on the porch last night and watched the skies turn dark as the thunder and lighting loomed closer, I kept remembering how the boys and I always did that before a storm. There was definitely a silence between Matt and myself. We both knew what was missing from the moment. It was sharing it with Michael.

I have this feeling that we're going to have a lot of moments like that in the days, weeks and months to come. As much as I'd like to say that I'm not looking forward to those moments, I can't. I'm actually kind of anxious for them. It's sad, but it also feels good to remember a special moment with Michael. I've been so afraid lately that I might forget something about him, but I realize now that I never will. I think that memories will be triggered just when God knows that I need them. I have faith that He will never let me forget anything about my Michael.

What I think I need to learn to do, is accept those memories with grace, happiness and joy, instead of the "I miss Michael, so I'm going to feel sorry for myself" attitude I've been having. After all, we've been saying that God gave us 18 wonderful years with Michael. I want to look at them from now on in that good light.

Yes, I'm sad. I'm always sad that we don't have Michael with us any longer. I'll forever be sad about that. But I don't want that sadness to shadow all the good I do have in my life. Next time there's a storm heading our way, and Matt and I sit outside waiting for its arrival, I want to remember fondly how it used to be, and cherish the way it is now.

Wednesday, May 31, 2006

We picked out a headstone for Michael today. And we found a company that makes them all on our own! Imagine that! (Still bitter about that company that solicited us the other day.) During the decision of what to put on it. I only cried once. Things are looking up!

I talked to a few people on the phone today, and again, hardly cried. We continue to discover, daily, the impact Michael has had on people, both before and after his death. Some of his bull riding buddies want to honor him by wearing a special sticker on their vests this year. People who admittedly don't know us or Michael, are writing, calling and e-mailing with their thanks to us for making Michael an organ donor.

I'm so grateful for all of the wonderful memories people have been sharing with us about their relationships with Michael. And I'm even more grateful to hear stories of young people who have begun to change their lives after seeing what has happened to Michael. But, boy, does temptation have a strong hold on our kids. I heard about an unfortunate incident after another local area town's graduation last weekend, where there was a party, with alcohol, and a lot of kids were arrested. Fortunately, as I've been told, there were at least a couple of White River kids there who had not been drinking (after being tested by the highway patrol) and were asked to drive many of the kids home. Amazing, isn't it. A neighboring town lost a young girl earlier this spring, and White River just lost Michael, and kids from both these towns (and others, I'm sure) still dare to chance their lives. Are their classmate's deaths not still fresh in their minds?

Kids – we couldn't wake Michael up in the hospital because

he was unconscious with severe brain damage. As far as I know, if you're reading this or any other news articles about him and his death, or were able to attend his funeral, you're not unconscious, nor do you have severe brain damage. So, what's you're excuse? Wake up!

God be with all of us.

Wednesday, May 31, 2006

Today is the last day of May. I'm sure glad this month is over. Certain months are just designed to make you think of certain events; December – Christmas; October – Halloween. April is a huge month for birthdays in the Glynn family. And now, May will always be remembered by me as the month Michael died.

I'm going back to work tomorrow. Today I kind of started. I went over to Martin and Mission to get some paperwork. The drive was nice. I listened to CD's that Michael burned of some of his favorite songs. He used to make a new one about every month. I wasn't surprised to hear that a lot of his favorites are also mine. When I was a teenager, I sure didn't like the same kind of music that my parents did. It made me feel comfortable, realizing that although we were of different generations, we shared a lot of common likes.

Michael loved Chris LeDoux songs. We've had Chris LeDoux tapes in our house since before Michael was born, even before Chris LeDoux became a household name. One of his songs is called *Addicted to an 8 Second Ride*. All the time on the road today let my mind wander. I kept thinking about Michael also being addicted to an eight second ride, and the correlation that has been made with his organ donations saving eight lives. I started taking the number eight with him further. Michael's accident occurred eight miles west of town. Michael was born in August, the eighth month. Michael passed away on the 17th – 1 plus 7 equals 8, in the year 2006 – 2 plus 6 equals 8. There would probably be more if I searched. This was probably a silly thing to do, but my mind works in strange ways anymore.

We are talking about sponsoring a buckle in memory of Michael at a few rodeos, beginning next year. While thinking about that I remembered something that happened to Michael a couple of years ago. It was at a high school practice rodeo. He won the buckle, and a lady came over to him afterwards, telling him that she sponsored the buckle in memory of a lost loved one. Well, Michael told me that she was acting kind of sad and all, so he asked her if she wanted the buckle back. She said yes, so he gave it to her.

When a couple of his friends wanted to see the buckle, he told them what happened. When he told me, I was kind of shocked. I thought it was odd that the lady wanted the buckle that she had sponsored. But, Michael didn't seem to mind. One of the other kids must have told the club advisor, because about two months later, the advisor sent Michael a replacement buckle, with a note thanking him for being so considerate to the sponsor. This event was proof that good deeds come back around!

More baby steps for our family today. The day after Michael's funeral, Roger and Matt moved some cows and calves. Matt rode Sox, the horse he's been riding a lot this spring. His saddle is getting kind of small for him, though, and Roger told him he could use Michael's saddle, and ride Michael's horse, Bandit, too. Bandit is a great horse. Matt wouldn't do it. He snuggled into his own saddle again, and rode Sox. Today, Roger and Matt went to a branding, and he rode Bandit. He's not ready to sit in Mikey's saddle, but he seems to be accepting his horse. I've been worried about Matt lately because he's such a quiet kid, and like most macho country boys, doesn't talk about his feelings. I took this act today as a good sign. My worry odometer went down a point!

Chapter 2

Thursday, June 1, 2006

I'm getting a lot of e-mails every single day, from people telling me how strong of a person they think I am because of what I've been writing in this journal. I think they're wrong. I have never felt so weak and vulnerable in my life. The smallest things bother me now. Comments that are a normal part of conversation sometimes bother me. They can leave me speechless, and everyone knows I'm not a speechless person! Michael's death has left me totally out of control; again, something that doesn't suit me well. I went back to work today, and I was at my desk when I heard a very loud vehicle pull up across the street. As soon as I heard it, I thought it was Michael and Jerod stopping by to spend their lunch hour at the office with me. It sounded just like Michael's branding car, the "old brown boat." Of course it wasn't. For just a split second, I thought I was waking up from this endless nightmare.

Last night Roger rolled over in bed, and his elbow hit my nose. It really stung, and I immediately thought of Michael. They said he probably broke his nose in the accident. I started to worry, wondering if he felt any pain from that, or any injuries for that matter, while he was laying in the ditch waiting to be found. I had to be near him, so once again I went to his room to cuddle up in his bed. This has worked in the past – being able to smell him on his sheets and clothes. But it didn't work last night. His scent is leaving the room. As hard as I've tried to keep it there (I don't open the windows, and seldom open the door), it is dissipating. I cried myself to sleep in there anyway.

Roger and Matt branded at a neighbor's this afternoon, and I decided to go out and help/visit with everyone. On my way out of town I was drawn to the cross on Michael's grave and pulled into the cemetery. I spent a while there, just sitting. It's a feeling I can't even describe. Michael was only six feet from me, yet I couldn't touch him. And I will never be able to, again.

During supper after the branding, a couple of the guys were

talking about chasing coyotes. I could only think of something Michael and Matt did last winter. Michael still had a broken bone in his ankle, but we just had a snowstorm so the boys took off on their snowmobiles. They didn't have a gun with them, but they found a coyote and decided to chase it. Michael ran over it (I know, I guess that's illegal – but what's anyone going to do to him for it now). He was pretty sure it was dead, but he said he wanted to bring it home to show his dad, and didn't want to lay it on the snowmobile behind him in case it wasn't really dead and jumped up on him. So they boys tied it up and tied the rope to the back of the snowmobile. Then they headed home. When they came through the yard, Roger was looking out the window of the house and just burst out laughing. Michael was going about as fast as he could, and the coyote was literally air-borne on the rope, about 10 feet behind. It looked like he was trying to fly a kite. Roger went outside and checked out Michael's trophy. It took them a long time to get the rope off; the knot was pulled too tight from the flight! Michael talked about how much fun he had that afternoon for a long time.

Someone said the other day that God didn't cause Michael's accident, but He is sure using him and his accident now. I agree. We have changed our lives, our faith has become even stronger, and I hear from people every day who are doing the same because of what happened to Mikey. It is this Faith in God's plan, Hope for good things to happen, and the Love of all of our friends (old and new friends), that keeps me going now. I keep saying that I'm taking baby steps in dealing with the loss of Michael. I know I'm moving forward, even if I go back a step once in a while. Some days I take three steps forward to make up for it! If we can all help to change the world the same way, God will smile!

Friday, June 2, 2006

Looking back, yesterday was certainly an "I'm feeling sorry for myself today" kind of day. Today was better. I spent the day working. It was very quiet and I got a lot of work caught up on. I wasn't as distracted there by thoughts and memories.

46

I've thought tonight about some of the things people have written to us. A lot of them start with, "you don't know me, but my son/daughter rodeoed with Michael." If they have a son, they will usually tell about Michael talking to them and helping their son behind the chutes some place. If they have a daughter, they say she always told them how good looking he was. Some have been pretty descriptive!

It all makes me wish I had one do-over. On graduation day I was so mad at him and one of his friends. They showed up at 2:45 instead of 2:00 for the class picture. Commencement started at 3:00. I didn't think they were going to get there at all. From then on, everything went according to schedule, and I hugged him and told him how proud I was when the class presented their parents with a flower. The reception was nice, and we took a lot of family photos. Thank God. Little did we know they would be the very last we would ever take of him. If I had known, I would still be taking pictures.

Afterwards we all went to Roger's parents house, so he could open some gifts. Before he left for the night, the last thing we told him was to not come home until the next afternoon. We knew they'd have a senior party and be out all night, and drinking. We wanted him to stay in town until he was good and awake, and sober. We'll never know exactly why he decided to go ahead and come home early the next morning, but it sure wasn't expected by us.

I wish I wouldn't have been mad at him earlier that day. I really wish we had been more specific with him that night. I wish we had told him how much everyone who ever met him loved him, and that he had a beautiful future waiting for him. I wish we had told him how we pictured him as an adult – happy with all of his dreams having come true! And how all of this would end if he got in his car and drove after he'd been drinking.

But, we weren't specific enough, and now he is gone.

I wish we had tried more. When Michael was in the hospital, everyone would say that they weren't giving up hope for his re-covery. No matter how old Michael was, or became, I wish we hadn't given up telling him of the dangers in the world.

It's easy to say that he made the choice, because we raised him to be able to make choices. We knew he had made bad choices with drinking before, but we just thought he'd grow out of them. Temptation and peer pressure to do wrong come from evil. When our kids are little we keep them away from bad things and bad people. Why do we stop when they turn that magical age of 18?

God gives us free will, much the same as we give kids choices. But God doesn't just ignore it when we make bad choices. I think he teaches us lessons from those choices. And He never gives up hoping that we'll make the right choices, and teaches us how. As parents, no matter what age our kids are, I think we need to keep parenting them and rearing them by example. God doesn't tell us that drinking is bad, then turn around and glorify it, or drink it Himself.

Sunday, June 4, 2006

This weekend was the first weekend of the High School Regional rodeos. We spent yesterday in Winner, where we presented Michael's bull riding vest and a Bible to one of his close friends. We wanted to give him the vest because it protected Michael in the arena, and the Bible because it protected him everywhere else. Another bull rider and friend of Michael's had his mom design a sticker in memory of Michael. It had a picture of a bucking bull overlapping a cross, and said *"In memory of Michael Glynn, 1987-2006."* She had dozens of them made for all the bull riders to wear on their vests. A lot more of the kids requested one, too, to put on their gear bags, rope bags, and even their horse trailers. She also sent a bunch of them to Wall for the kids in that region's rodeo to have. Truly amazing! Raven Angus and the Petersek family sponsored the bull riding average buckle this year, but were very thoughtful and had the words *In Memory of Michael Glynn* engraved on the back. Another good friend carried the Stars and Stripes in honor of Michael.

I did pretty well until the anthem was finished and he rode solemnly past where I was standing. It was hard. But the most difficult part of the day was when they turned a bull out for Michael. I know that doing so is a wonderful tribute, but it was very, very hard to see that bull come out of the chute, without Michael on him.

Some people said they didn't see how we could be there. Being there was easy. We feel very at-home and comfortable at any rodeo; after all, that's where we've practically lived every weekend of the summer for the past ten years! It's just not the same without Michael there. But then, what is anymore. A lot of the kids told us they feel the same way. My heart aches for all of them.

A very strange thing happened as we were getting ready to leave for Winner. I have a necklace with a depiction of St. Christopher, the Patron Saint of Safe Travels, on it. Ever since I receive the necklace, I have worn it at every single rodeo I was at with Michael. Just before the bull riding, I would always grasp the pendant and say a prayer for Michael to have eight seconds of safe travels. Saturday morning I decided to go ahead and wear it, but the chain broke when I was putting it on. So I put it in my pocket, and right before the rodeo, held it in my hand and asked in a prayer for safe travels in the arena for everyone that day.

It was good to be in Winner, but kind of exhausting emotionally. We didn't go back on Sunday, but will try to be at the state finals in Belle Fourche in a few weeks.

Last night we had dinner with some friends. Late in the evening I was able to get some feelings off my chest that I've been too afraid to say out loud or write about. I felt so relieved afterwards. It was mostly about the guilt I've been feeling. I knew I was wrong to think what I had been thinking, but it felt good to have these wonderful friends reassure me.

Finally, today, I felt a little bit rejuvenated. I was able to start writing thank you notes to people who sent flowers, memorials, food, and helped us in so many ways the past few weeks.

It's about 8:30 p.m. now, on Sunday night. It was almost precisely this time, three weeks ago, that I spoke to my son for the last time. Actually, I still talk to him often, but it was the last time he was able to speak back to me. I can't even begin to comprehend eternity, because the past 21 days seem like they've been an eternity. I miss Michael so incredibly much!

Please, God, be with us as we continue to travel through the rest of our life on earth.

Monday, June 5, 2006

Roger is in Michael's room right now, going through a bunch of pictures. We're going to have a couple of photos put on the headstone at the cemetery, and we have to pick them out tonight. Michael's bedroom is exactly how he left it, the normal mess, along with all of the pictures and his buckles that we had displayed at the graduation reception, and later at the funeral. Clothes are scattered on the floor, the bed hasn't been made, and now there are a couple of boxes of pictures we're going through.

I don't like Roger being in there, so I had to leave. I know, he's his father, and has every right to be there, and should be there, but I'm having trouble right now having someone else touching and going through Michael's things. If I had just cleaned up and organized things in his room by now, I could have just handed Roger a nice little stack of whatever he was looking for. But I didn't. So Roger's looking himself, and it's almost more than I can stand.

I guess it's partly because I've had this fixation on Michael's room and the smell that's in there. I've spent quite a few nights sleeping in Michael's bed lately, just to engulf myself in his smell, trying to be closer to him, and never forget. Most nights it's very hard to sleep, and I get the most rest when I curl up in his bed. I'm just not ready for anyone else to be in there.

Finally, Roger found the pictures he was looking for, the decision has been made with which one to use, and he's gone. I'm not ready to pack Michael's things away yet, but I'm pretty sure that I'm going to be cleaning and organizing his room this weekend. I don't want to do this again.

Three weeks ago, tonight, we didn't know Michael was going to die. We went to the hotel in Sioux Falls thinking that he would be awake when we went back the next morning. How can you go from a graduation celebration one night, to arguing about a photo for your son's headstone, in just 22 days?

Dear God, this is too hard. Please, give me strength.

Tuesday, June 6, 2006

The "what ifs" have plagued me lately. But now I've found some "what ifs" that I think are blessings.

I've thought a lot about just how Michael died. Yes, the easy answer is that it was the end result of drinking, driving, speeding and not wearing a seat belt. But there seem to have been a lot of teenage accidents the mirrored Michael's accident. Except for a few things.

What if Michael had died at the scene of the accident? He didn't, so we, and many of his friends, were able to say goodbye to him. We spent 2 1/2 days with him, holding his hands, talking to him, praying for him, before he died. It was having this time that allowed the doctors to keep his organs functioning so that upon his death he could be an organ donor.

When they first told us that his brain damage was worsening, I was preparing myself for a lifetime of caring for him. I was ready to bathe him, dress him, feed him - whatever it took for the rest of my life, just to have him alive and with me. But that wouldn't have been the kind of life Michael would have wanted. What if that had that been the future scenario? I would have had his body with me, but his spirit would have been gone. And Michael's spirit was his life.

What if Michael had had someone in the car with him? What if they would have died, and he survived? I don't think he could have lived with that. I know I couldn't have.

What if he had hit an oncoming car? And the same thing – others died, or others and not him.

What if he had never accepted Jesus Christ as his Savior? I shudder at the thought of that.

It was such a horrible tragedy, but there are still blessings to be found.

By the way, I talked to Roger last night about my problem with him being in Michael's room. I told him that it was my problem, and I realize it, but that it still bothered me. He really seemed to respect what I said with genuine understanding. Or, maybe he's just lived with me long enough, that even now he accepts my craziness! I think it's good that we talked about it last night. I think we both have a lot of things we want to say to each other about Michael's accident, but are kind of scared to. I know I do. But if we keep working through things slowly, at some point I think we'll get there. And when we do, we'll be able to handle the conversation with love and understanding.

Each day brings a new set of struggles.

Each day brings sunlight and renewed life.

Wednesday, June 7, 2006

We got the first hospital bill from Michael's accident today. The air ambulance from Rosebud to Sioux Falls alone cost $8,225. I was shocked. Thankfully we have insurance. I don't know what people do without it. Hospital bills aren't new to us this year. Michael had a number of accidents the past year – bull stepped on his knee, broken ankle, the prairie dog hunting shooting accident. We started taking them in stride, and even laughing about them. The hospital bills didn't seem so bad, because we always brought him home afterward. But with this hospital bill, it's just another reminder that he didn't come home.

It also reminded me of the hospital bill when he was born.

We brought Michael home on a weekend, when there was no one in the hospital business office. Roger stopped at the office though, and had this bewildered look on his face. He said, "What do we do now?" Then I got the bewildered look. He said, "They won't let us take him without paying the bill first, will they?" I laughed so hard. I remember asking him what he thought they would do with our baby if we asked to make payments on the bill.

It seems like that was yesterday. Yet it was a lifetime ago. It was Mikey's lifetime ago.

Thursday, June 8, 2006

I drove by a hayfield on my way home from town today.

We're not putting up hay this year. It started out extremely sparse, and then a hailstorm went through and made the decision for us. There will be no hay this year for us. I think that's for the best, considering. For the past six years Roger and both boys have been haying together. Matt has done all the raking, while Roger and Michael switched off between cutting and baling. I'm glad Roger and Matt don't have to be in the hayfield this year, going round and round and spending all day thinking Michael will be over the next hill.

I remember the first year Michael helped hay. He was about nine years old, and Roger started him out raking two windrows into one. Roger said that he made sure Michael was always in the same field he was, and kept a pretty close eye on him. He said that every time Michael would go around a corner, he would stop for a minute, get off the tractor, and walk behind it. At first he thought Michael was broke down, but he quickly got back on and took off. Next corner, same thing. Then Roger thought he was just taking a nature break, quite often though. When it happened again he drove over to see if Michael was sick or something. As it turned out, when going around the corners, he was leaving about a three foot length of hay from getting picked up and moved to the new windrow. Michael was stopping each time and walking back to pick it up by hand and move it to the windrow. Roger was one proud daddy that day!

I sat at the cemetery for a while after work today. The cross Roger built is so beautiful. I don't even want a headstone for Michael now. It's a good thing we've got one ordered, or I'd probably put off getting one for a long time.

It's just not supposed to be this way. I can't imagine not watching Michael grow older. I can't imagine not seeing him get married, and holding his babies someday. Like a friend told me the day we put the cross on his grave, this whole thing just sucks!

Friday, June 9, 2006

I became a stalker today.

I had a hard time working, so I took the afternoon off. I went to Valentine to pay the funeral home bill and get the order for Michael's headstone finalized. Talk about a bad kind of shopping spree! Later, I was in the grocery store when I looked up and saw a young man that reminded me so much of Michael that my heart almost stopped!

He was the same height, with dark hair and a tanned face and arms. He was wearing jeans with the legs half tucked into his boots. He had on a white t-shirt; the front tucked in by his buckle, the rest hanging out. He was wearing a cap that was visibly mixed with sweat and grease. And he had on an ivory beaded necklace (might be called something different for guys – seems strange to say my son wore a necklace!) just like Michael used to wear! His face was a little different, obviously. His nose was softer, and his cheeks were fuller. He had dark eyes, but no one could ever have Michael's eyes. Michael had the biggest, brownest eyes, with the longest eye lashes. So I avoided looking at this boy's face. From behind he was a ringer for my Michael.

Then I did something I can't believe I did. I followed him. I just couldn't stop looking!

His gait was a slightly shorter than Michael's, but still very close. He had that same casual "swing" when he walked. I followed him to the check-out, where he apparently knew the high school aged cute little clerks and the carry-out boy. They all started talking and teasing each other. This boy looked like he just came from the hayfield, and I wanted to ask him if he was going back, and should I make him a lunch to take along, or bring sandwiches out to him later. But I didn't. I just watched him.

He bought a package of string cheese, a bag of nacho chips and a Mountain Dew. He needed jerky. Michael would have bought jerky instead of the cheese. Then he left. And I was standing in the check-out line with half of my groceries.

So I paid for what I had and left. He wasn't in the parking lot when I got outside. I wish I could have closed my eyes and somehow been able to touch that boy's arm.

Saturday, June 10, 2006

God blessed us tonight, and gave us an opportunity to start healing. We had a light rain and some thunder roll through, and the electricity was off for almost four hours. I believe God was saying, here guys, I'm giving you an opportunity to talk, with no excuses. Thank God, we listened.

I've been very angry with Roger the past couple of days. I've been completely blaming him for Michael having died. I decided that he hadn't been strict enough with Michael, and allowed him to do too many things, and stay out too late, etc., etc., etc. I've been telling myself that if Roger had done things differently, Michael might still be alive today. Then the electricity went out. There was no TV, no computer, no radio, and no lights. So, I did what is seldom done in the 21st century, I opened up a book (next to the window – read until it got took dark to see). It's called Roses In December and is a book dealing with grief. About halfway through I got to a part talking about how to deal with anger.

Basically, someone wrote that they used so much energy, and were so tired, because of having this constant anger. I thought, that's me! I kept reading, and praying - something I've also neglected the past couple of days. Pretty soon it was too dark to even read, so I went into the living room where Roger was and just sat. Eventually I told him that I'd been mad at him, and why. I also told him that I just couldn't be mad at him any longer. I found out that I wasn't nearly as mad at him, as he's been at himself. We talked for a very long time about that anger, and the guilt we've each been carrying around.

Tonight was definitely a move forward.

And from The Book, *The Bible*: Eph. 4:31.32: Let all bitterness, and wrath, and anger, and clamor, and evil speaking, be put away from you, with all malice: And be ye kind one to another, tenderhearted, forgiving one another, even as God for Christ's sake hath forgiven you.

Thank you God, for the rain, no electricity, forgiving us of our sins, and showing us how to love and forgive others - and ourselves.

Sunday, June 11, 2006

I said I was going to straighten up Michael's room this weekend, and I think I went a little overboard. At least, compared to what I had intended to do. I did straighten things up, and in the process, packed some things away, and threw some things away. Decisions are hard right now. What do you do with his socks and underwear? Matt doesn't want Michael's blue jeans, let alone such personals as socks and underwear. I suppose the right thing to do would have been to send them to Goodwill or the Salvation Army. But I don't think I could do that. I'll give them a monetary donation instead to ease my guilt. I packed some clothes up to take to the dump.

I'm still keeping the shirts though. I haven't decided yet, but I'm considering making them into a quilt, maybe a couple of quilts. Michael was very proud that he made it on the Wrangler All Star team last year, so we had him buried in the shirt he got for that honor. When I saw kids wearing that same shirt in Winner last weekend I kept thinking – hey, Michael has a shirt like that . . . and now he's buried in it.

Weird, isn't it. I'm completely okay with someone else using his heart and lungs, but I don't want anyone else wearing his socks and blue jeans.

I found a box in Michael's closet that has the words "Ya better stay the hell out of here, ya hear" on the top of it. When I opened it, I knew immediately why he wanted us to not know what was in there. There were some really sentimental things inside. He probably thought keeping those things made him seem less tough. There were Little Britches bumper stickers full of pins and memorabilia from various rodeos. There were newspaper clippings of him riding. There was a clipping from an article in the LBR newsletter last year about an 18-year-old bull rider from Michigan that died after a bull stepped on him at a rodeo. And, there was a folded sheet of paper that made me cry more than anything else I found. It simply said, in his handwriting – 2006 Goals, *SD High School state champ, *Qualify for the NHSRA Finals, *Qualify for SDRA Finals, *Get SDRA Rookie Cowboy, *Qualify for NBRT Finals,

*Finish top 5 in NBRT, *Win 5,000 dollars in 2006, *2006 4-h state champ, *Get a rodeo scholarship.

I know Michael could have reached every one of these goals. And now, to think that he won't get the chance, all because of a decision to drive home after he'd been drinking that night. It gives me a sick feeling in the pit of my stomach, and makes my legs feel like rubber.

I showed Roger what I had saved, and what I didn't. He didn't have a problem with anything I decided. It didn't even bother me that he came into the room and started touching and holding Michael's things. Michael's room is far from empty. But now everything is in kind of an order. It's starting to feel a little less like "Mikey's room", but I still need it to take a little longer before it's just another room in the house.

Other than that it's been a "too quiet" weekend. Roger said once today that Michael sure kept us entertained on the weekends! We made hotel reservations for the state finals today. It was another normal thing to do. I just can't believe that we won't be going there with him, or going there to watch him ride. It is just so unreal, still.

Monday, June 12, 2006

I think I'm going to stop posting journal entries on this website. It has been good for me to write about my feelings each day, and I will likely continue, but I think I'll just do it privately from now on. By posting my feelings here, it has allowed me to hear comments from so many people – many of our friends, and many others who only new Michael. I treasure all of the memories everyone has shared with us. I really had no idea that Michael had touched so many lives.

Whenever I was feeling really bad, or having a bad day, it definitely helped me to read positive messages from everyone.

Today was another one of those not-so-good days. But I was listening to the radio on the way home tonight, and a song was played called *God Only Cries For The Living*. The words to that song rang so true to me. It was sad, but I only have to barely try, and I can find sadness in so many things any more. But the words of the song were also uplifting to me. I do believe, God only cries for us, those living here on earth. And our tears are also for ourselves. We really shouldn't be crying for Michael, and maybe we really aren't. We're crying for ourselves, because our lives are going to be emptier without him. I think it's going to be very important for me to constantly try to remember that Michael's life is wonderful now. We thought he had a great life here, but remember, it's nothing compared to his life now. I want so badly to not feel sorry for myself any longer. I want to rejoice about Michael now being with God.

I think that the closer we get to God, the more evil tries to intervene. Selfishness, anger and hatred are born of evil, not from the love of God. I will not let evil prevail. God will be with me, helping me along the way, if I just ask. And boy, am I asking!

So, as I finish this entry tonight, I again send my warmest and most sincere thanks to all of you who are still with our family in thought and prayer. We're not in this alone, either. Please continue to pray for our healing, as I will for all of you.

Mikey's spirit is living with God now, but his memory will live in our hearts forever. Thank you, everyone, for loving and caring about Michael!!

God bless each of you, always.

Tuesday, June 13, 2006

I think I'm going to use my woman's prerogative to change my mind, and continue writing in this journal's web site a little longer.

I couldn't believe when I got home tonight – the number of e-mails from people saying they understood my quitting, but wished I wouldn't. Many said it's helped them deal with their own emotions surrounding Michael's death. Didn't I say yesterday that we're all in this together–to help each other through? So maybe it's just selfish of me to stop. After all, I am planning on writing my thoughts each day anyway, so why not here.

Plus, I had a wonderful visit today with a very good friend.

He, too, reminded me that God did not cause Michael's accident and death, but was going to use it for some very good things. We talked about the good that we've already seen come from his death. I don't want that to ever stop.

I've had so, so many of you e-mail me after reading my journal here, saying that you or your child's life is changing for the better because of what happened to Michael. Dozens have said they're not allowing alcohol in their homes anymore, and those who have talked about Michael's funeral service especially move me.

The message of salvation that was given to everyone at the funeral was most definitely God using Michael's death for the good of all of us. Even people who couldn't make it to the funeral have told me that they heard about it. That means people are talking about salvation, and I believe that it also means people are accepting Christ into their lives. If this is how God is using my child's death for a good cause, then praise Him! What a wonderful tribute that alone is to Michael – to know that through Michael, God is sending His message of grace and salvation to so many lives!

And here we've been impressed with all the lives Michael touched when he was alive! There is no comparison to the lives he is touching now, and with our help and with God walking with us, the number of lives and souls that will continue to be saved! It just makes my broken heart swell with pride, and in turn, slowly start to mend. I think our hearts will always carry the scar of Michael's death, but if we stay focused on God and His word, we will be able to go on.

When Michael was in the hospital, I asked everyone to not stop praying for a miracle, for him to be healed. I believe what Pastor Jackie said at the funeral service; our prayers were answered, with a "yes." Michael was healed. He is healed in Heaven, not on earth, as we wanted him to be. And as I've said before, spending eternity in Heaven with Jesus Christ is a miracle! God's will was done, and our prayers were answered!

So I'm going to ask everyone to continue praying with me now. And I'm going to try from now on to focus on praying; yes, for specifics; but for God's will to be done. I'm asking God to use me, and Michael's memory, to help change the world around me. Please ask God the same thing yourself, and between us, more than 10,000 angels will be with us!

Wednesday, June 14, 2006

I have had such a splitting headache all day today, and nothing is helping. It was a pretty mundane, not-much-to-think-about day at work, too.

It's been about a week since I felt like I needed to fall asleep in Michael's room, but last night I did. I also opened the windows in there last night, for the first time. Michael's smell is still there, but it's getting fainter. I finally decided it couldn't hurt that much to let some fresh air in. I fell asleep right away, but woke up about 5 a.m. from a horrible nightmare. I won't even go into the details, but it had to do with Michael's funeral.

I remember waking up and not being able to move. I looked at the open windows and felt like there was something trying to get in, and that I should close them. But I couldn't move. It was the most horrible feeling. So, I started praying. Pretty soon I was thanking God for being so close to me. I truly believe that the closer we get to God, the harder evil tries to intervene. I think the nightmare I had last night, and feeling like I did, was evil. Must mean that something is being threatened by my Faith in God, even through this real nightmare we're living each day. That actually makes me feel kind of good!

Anyway, I think the whole ordeal early this morning is what gave me the headache today. And amazingly, after coming home tonight, and writing this down – I feel better already.

One month ago was graduation day. I wonder if we'll ever stop remembering these daily, weekly and monthly anniversaries of the events surrounding Michael's accident and death.

Thursday, June 15, 2006

I don't think we intend to lie when people ask, "how are you." I think it's just so much easier to say, "good, how are you." Then they say, "fine." And the conversation ends. Well, here goes the truth today.

"I feel lousy."

"I have a headache that is making me feel sick."

"Life is not fair."

"I want to reverse time."

"I feel like I'm suffocating."

"This can't be real."

Saturday, June 17, 2006

June 17. Michael died exactly one month ago.

Things I've read about people who have lost a loved one say that the events and days were a haze, and they don't ever remember much about them.

I think I remember every detail of those days.

May 17 was a Wednesday. The morning started off like the day before, with us at the hospital. The doctors told us the day before that Michael could go on like he was for a week, or even a month. They were sure death was inevitable, but weren't sure how long it would be before his brain hemorrhaged. On Wednesday morning, they told us that they were sure it would happen before that day was over. They had tried all night to drain the fluid on his brain, and in doing so, he also lost a lot of other body fluids. That's what the medicine they were giving him was doing. His brain was not functioning enough to make the medicine work only where it was needed. When his body started to dehydrate, they had to start giving him fluids back. The doctors said that this was to be expected very near the end.

Of course, at one point Michael moved, which he hadn't done in nearly 24 hours. It gave us hope. Sometimes since, we've thought of it as false hope. But I think that was wrong. There can't be anything such as 'false' hope. Hope is hope, plain and simple. The movement Michael made was actually a reflex action that happened as soon as his brain began to hemorrhage. When Roger and I realized what was really happening, we asked the nurse to not let anyone else in the room with him. So the rest of the family and all his friends stayed in the waiting room and hoped, while

Roger and I spent the last four hours of Michael's life, alone with him, holding his hand, and loving him.

Even today, as I write this, my eyes are filled with tears. But I feel like I'm back there in that hospital room with him, holding his hand, and loving him.

I remember his friends coming to check on Michael a couple of times, as did Amber. We told them everything was the same, which it was. What they thought of as the same, and what we knew was the same, just weren't the same thing.

I'm not sure how they did it – I heard some of the kids went to Mitchell, or someone came from Mitchell, or it was e-mailed – but the kids somehow made a CD of Michael's favorite song – Colby Yates singing *Headin' To The Rodeo*. We asked the nurse get a CD player and we played the song for Michael in his room. It still seems very fitting that this is what he was listening to at the end of his life.

I'm glad I remember all these details of that day. It was the worst day of my life, and likely always will be. Michael's body was hooked up to machines, he had tubes in his mouth and nose and IV tubes in his arms, but I don't care. To the rest of the world, he may have looked just like another dying patient, but to me, he was the world. (I'll explain that little song-like play on words another time – another story about a joke Michael played on me one day). But it's true. He looked perfect to me that day, just like he did every other day since he was born.

I have to remember everything about him and his life – both the good and the bad days, and the horrible last day, because all of them were him. It took everything about him, the good and the bad, to make him what he was – wonderful and perfect, at least to me. And if we don't have a few bad days, we wouldn't appreciate the good days as much either.

Now, when I think I'm having a bad day, I can remember back to the day he died. And today isn't quite so bad anymore.

Sunday, June 18, 2006

Well, we made it through yesterday. I took a nap in the afternoon. I prayed so hard that I would be able to sleep, and I did. I did not want to be awake at 2:36 p.m., the time Michael was pronounced dead. I woke up feeling pretty good.

Roger and Matt have dedicated their "no-haying-this-year" summer to tearing down a couple of old buildings we have on the place, and building a new horse barn. It won't be large, but it will serve our needs. They seem excited about it and it's good to see them doing something productive. Roger and I have had a hard time wanting to actually do anything the past few weeks. I think it's good they have this project to work on that will take some time to finish. It will give them focus. I, of course, still have the job of writing thank-you cards for all the memorials and gifts people sent in honor of Michael. I don't know why, because it's not a hard job, but I can't seem to get it done. I just keep finding excuses to put it off. I'm usually fairly good at handling things, but now I'm finding that some of the simplest things get blown way out of proportion by me.

All of Michael's finances were in my name, along with his, except one little $50 savings bond. When I went to cash it in, I found that I would have to provide a certified copy of his death certificate, which costs $10, and would take a couple of weeks to get. I didn't want to do it. I thought about just forgetting it and letting someone else figure it out in 30 or 40 years. Getting another copy of the death certificate is not a big deal. The funeral home obtained two for us, and we have one left. I could give the bank that one, and call the courthouse and get another, or just call and order another for the bank. But I just can't do it now. I want these things done! But I just can't get them finished! On my way out of the bank that day I thought I was going to be sick. Now I keep thinking – why can't I just handle this simple little job? It's easy, and I deal with many, much larger financial decisions every day. Maybe I just need to hold on to some things. Maybe I don't really want it all to be finished.

Yesterday when Roger and Matt were working I went out to see them. We were picking up nails and such from one of the old buildings so I could mow around the new bare space. I must have been out there for about an hour, and all of a sudden it occurred to me that I hadn't thought of Michael for that whole hour. It kind of felt good. But then I felt so, so bad. I don't want to not think about him, yet I want to think about something else. When I do think about something else, I feel guilty that I haven't thought about him constantly. I am so terrified that I will forget something about him, either now or 30 years from now, and I can't stand the thought of that happening.

My aunt e-mailed me this morning, and told of a poem that my cousin told her about. In the poem, it says that when you lose a husband you become a widower, when you lose a wife you become a widow, and when you lose a parent you become an orphan. But when you lose a child, you have no name, just unbearable pain. My God, that is so true! I feel nameless, and empty.

Monday, June 19, 2006

There isn't a day that goes by that I don't hear from someone with a story about Michael. Today I was blessed to hear many of them. To be honest with you, for a while I was kind of jealous when I heard stories about Michael from people who were strangers to me. I thought – I wish I had spent all of his time with him. I miss him and I wish I could have kept him to myself. I thought – if I had known that he was going to die at age 18, no matter what, I would have suffocated him with attention, and shared him with no one. Thankfully, that feeling is gone. Now, I'm very thankful he knew so many people and they thought so much of him. I always, always, always said, that he may have had a wild side, but at the end of the day he was a great kid. I'm so glad that's what other people saw in him too.

Parenting is hard work and there are no instruction manuals. When Michael died from an alcohol and speeding related car accident, I immediately thought I had failed as a parent. After all, it was my job to teach him not to do those things, and he did them anyway, and now he's gone. I know he's in a much better place, and like a friend said the other day, he wouldn't want to come back here. Heaven is too perfect. Still, I wanted him to live a long life here. I love my life. I have the best family and friends. I have everything I want or need. Of course, I went through the normal struggles to get to this place in life. And I want the same for all my kids. I wanted it for Michael.

Sometimes people say they wish their kids were little again, and there were certainly moments I had wished Michael was still a toddler, and a tad more controllable! But kids are such a tremendous joy to watch grow. I was so glad that Michael finally got through high school. He had been a straight A student through elementary and middle school. But about halfway through high school he decided he'd had enough of books. He thought he was ready to be an adult. We kind of gave him that inspiration, by what we taught him on the ranch. He could have practically run this place already.

I remember when he was about 12 years old; he virtually memorized the whole Angus Sire Summary book. When Roger would talk about a certain bull, and say who his sire and dam was, Michael could tell him their entire bloodlines, and most of their EPD information. And he was always right! He was growing up, and living his life. I, too, was ready for him to get through high school, and begin the next stage of his life. Now, it just breaks my heart that he muddled through high school, because he had to, and didn't have the chance to experience that next stage that he and I were both so looking forward to.

With all of my earthly goods, I would trade every single last thing, for just one more hour with Michael.

I still maintain that writing in this journal is about the most stable thing I do each day anymore. It's been good to have a place to release my thoughts. I know I say about the same thing all the time, and I think Roger kind of gets tired of hearing it from me. So, writing it here has been very good for me.

But I'm also doing it for another reason. I hope that all of Michael's friends, and other teenagers, will read this – my thoughts and feelings each day from having lost him. I'm really no different than your parents. If you choose to drink, drive, speed – your parents could be feeling the exact same way I am now. Please don't take that chance. Please don't take a risk that could cause you're parents to grieve losing you for the rest of their lives. I know for a fact that Michael never thought that this would happen to him. And I never thought it would happen to him, and us, either. But it can. It did. And it's just not worth it. Please, make wise choices. And above all, choose to let Jesus Christ live in your heart.

Tuesday, June 20, 2006

I sat down at my desk while supper was cooking, and told myself I was going to write some thank you notes. And here I am instead, writing in my journal. I just can't seem to get focused on those darned things. I think it was best that I handled a lot of things right away, soon after Michael's death and funeral. I think at that time I was so numb, that I was able to do those things, and not completely realize that they were being done. Now, I'm in an "I-don't-care-if-anything-gets-done" kind of stupor.

Right now it looks as though a storm may be moving our way. I have a wonderful view out my office window, looking to the northwest. I know it sounds silly, but I find myself watching clouds almost as much now as I did when I was a little kid. I remember how I loved to lay on the ground and find pictures of things in the clouds, just like all other kids do. It's been a few years since I've done that with my own kids, unless a shape really caught our attention. So, here I am again, acting very child-like, watching the clouds.

It was easy to believe, while growing up, that Heaven is up, and hell is down. I suppose that's why I'm infatuated with clouds again. I look up and wonder if somehow Michael is sitting on one, watching over all of us who love and miss him. I know if he is, God is right there with him. It makes me feel good, and calm. Sometimes lately I've noticed that my hands start shaking for absolutely no reason, and my heart starts beating faster and I feel short of breath. Watching the clouds helps tremendously.

Wednesday, June 21, 2006

Somebody died on the county road near our house a few years, the result of a car accident. Each year since, someone has brought a full can of beer and a pack of cigarettes and laid them in the ditch next to the place of the accident. I always found that to be disgusting, but thought well, to each his own.

I went to visit Michael's grave tonight after work, and found something that not only disgusted me, it just really pissed me off. Somebody put a cigarette butt next to the base of the cross. Michael didn't even smoke. He chewed, but did not smoke. Then, I found a knife stuck into the grave, near where his heart would be. There were also a few coins strewn around it. It wasn't a huge knife, but it wasn't a pocketknife either. I don't know if it was meant as a memorial, or something the opposite. Either way, I didn't like it, or the cigarette. I took the cigarette butt and the knife and the coins and threw them in the trunk of the car, then threw them in the garbage can at home. If these things were meant to be a memorial – why? They don't signify anything good at all, or anything about Michael. One thing I learned tonight – I will be stopping at Michael's gravesite each day I possibly can to make sure it does not get defaced again.

I just don't understand the mindset of people who would do something like that. What could it possibly accomplish to put cigarettes, beer and so forth on the place someone died, let alone on their grave?

Michael's grave is covered with flowers, boots with flower displays and stone tributes, along with a few roses and even a beautiful and simple cross necklace. I feel so good when I go there and see these things that other people who loved him have honored his gravesite with. To you who have left these things – thank you! They mean so much to me. I want to keep his gravesite looking beautiful all through the year, not just during Memorial Day. Thank you for helping!

As far as Michael's gravesite goes, Roger and I are the "to each his own" deciders. When I see things like I saw today, that simply disgust me, I'll continue to do as I did; they will be thrown in the trash. And I certainly hope I never hear of kids, or anyone, paying tribute to Michael with a drink, as I've heard of people doing sometimes. That would be the ultimate disgrace to him, and our family.

I have also decided today that losing Michael will never get easier. I don't care if it's 40 years from now; I know I'll feel the way I do today. I've thought before that it will never get better, but in time it will get easier. I know now that it's just not possible.

I worked in Mission today, and I cried constantly from the time I turned at the junction to the time I got to the cemetery in White River, and for no particular reason at all. After I left White River, I only cried about half way home. Some people might say this is normal, or a normal stage in the grieving process. But I disagree. There is no normal process for grieving. There is nothing normal at all anymore. Nothing will ever be normal again, because normal is having Michael in our lives.

I still can't believe this is real. It is so unfair.

Friday, June 23, 2006

I know for sure now that somebody is reading this journal. I went to Michael's gravesite tonight, and there was a can of chew on it. But more importantly, one of his classmates put their graduation tassel on the cross. It was beautiful. June 22 - Michael's body has been in it's new permanent home for one month.

Today had it's ups and downs. I had a visit from a good friend and we talked, remembered and cried together for a long time. Now I know why crying is good. It's a good release, and you feel so exhausted when you're done, that you just feel calm.

I also went to a little kid's baseball game to get some pictures of the kids for the paper. And who was there, but the person who bought the alcohol for the kids' graduation party this year. I could hardly stand it. I'm not embarrassed or afraid to say that I don't particularly like this person, never really did. Tonight it really bothered me that he was there. He was there, and Michael wasn't, isn't, never will be. I am SO, SO, SO incredibly tired of the people who buy alcohol for kids getting off without even a slap on the hand. And now, this one not only contributed to the delinquency of a minor, he contributed to the death of my child. I know I have to forgive him, and I am praying to, but I can't yet.

I pray that I am able to live a long life. But I'm also anxious to be able to ask God, why. I guess I just need to be patient. In the scheme of eternity, waiting a few decades for that answer doesn't seem so long.

Yes, I believe that God never gives us more than we can bear. I remember telling that to a friend of mine many years ago, when she lost her mother unexpectedly. Now I understand though. God gives us the means to be able to handle anything. God never gives us more than we can bear, but He also tells us that He will be there with us if we just ask. And God, obviously, can handle anything. So, if we remember to ask Him to be with us, we'll be able to bear anything. It seems so simple. So why did it take me so long, and losing a child, to finally "get it?"

Clouds. They're here in front of me again tonight. Watching. Thank you God.

Friday, June 23, 2006

South Dakota High School Rodeo Finals began today. Instead of being in Belle Fourche, I visited Michael again at his gravesite. I thought today about how proud I've been of Michael, and how proud I would have been at him at the finals this year. I thought that I wouldn't get to be proud of him now, or ever again. Then I realized – yes I can. When I think about the e-mails and letters I get from people who say they have changed their lives after Michael's death - even the fact that I have changed my life to much - well, it makes me very proud of Michael. I was very proud of the things Michael did and accomplished when he was alive. But I'm also proud of the things that are being accomplished through him in his death.

I also went to the Rosebud Hospital today and picked up a copy of his medical records from there. That's where he was taken first - before he was flown to Sioux Falls. I really can't believe he lived until Wednesday. For almost the first twenty minutes he was in Rosebud, his blood pressure was around 75/35. His temperature was 92 degrees. He was not doing very well. What everyone did to keep him alive until Wednesday just amazes me. You can't imagine how grateful I am of that. As horrible as it is that he died, I don't know how I could have handled it if he would have been gone by the time we got to Rosebud, or on the way to Sioux Falls, or even Monday night in Sioux Falls. The timing of everything gave his grandparents, dozens of his friends, and us the opportunity to see him and say goodbye. What an incredible blessing that was!

We're "headin' to the rodeo" tomorrow morning. We want to watch and support Tanner and Jerod tomorrow, and if all goes well they'll both make it to the short go on Sunday! We'll be there for that too. They're going to do something special before the short go performance on Sunday for Michael and another rodeo-family girl, who was also killed in a car accident earlier this spring. It will be nice. It will also be a very hard weekend. I'm going to be seeing Michael in my mind all day, and wishing I was for real. But - we need to be there for all of his friends.

Monday, June 26, 2006
It sure feels good to be home. We didn't get home last night until close to midnight. We had to stop in Rapid and pick up some new garage windows to replace the ones that broke when a hail storm whipped through our place last month.

We spent two entire days doing nothing much more than sitting in a grandstand watching rodeo performances, and driving to and from Belle Fourche, but we were completely exhausted from the trip. I'm sure it was 99 percent emotional and one percent physical.

Both Roger and I kind of tried to keep to ourselves during Saturday's two rodeos. I, for one, didn't really want to spend the day with the "how are you doing" and "we're so sorry for your loss" conversations. I know everyone means very well, but sometimes I just want to be alone and quiet. It was hard being at the state finals without Michael, but I really did try to focus on all the rest of the kids we were there cheering for. For the most part, I think we were able to do that.

Between the two performances on Saturday we checked into our motel room. I remember lying on the bed, closing my eyes, and thinking "okay, when I open my eyes, Michael is going to walk through the door, and this nightmare will end." Well, it didn't happen. I keep telling myself that we have to start realizing that this is real. But the 'uncomprehendable' is very hard to comprehend.

Sunday's short go performance – well, there really aren't words to describe the tribute that was paid to Michael and Jessica.

After the introduction of the sponsor's flags by members of the Wrangler All Star Team (of which Michael was a member), and the grand entry by all of the day's contestants, the tribute began.

Michael's best friend very slowly and solemnly rode into the arena leading a rider-less horse in honor of Michael. The horse was saddled and Michael's bull riding chaps were lying across it. The same was done by a friend of Jessica's, with a wreath on her saddle. Everyone on the grounds stood up and even removed their hats. It was so quiet you could hear a pin drop. I started crying as soon as they came in through the gate. Roger had wanted me to take a picture of it, but there was no way I could have. My eyes were a blur. As the boys led the horses in front of the grandstand, the announcer talked about Michael and Jessica and read their obituaries. Following them were all the rest of the contestants, on horseback. They all circled and ended up in the center of the arena as the announcer finished. Then they quietly followed the two empty-saddled horses, out of the arena.

It was the most moving tribute I have ever seen. I don't think there was anyone who wasn't crying. I didn't even try to stop. There would have been no point trying, it wouldn't have worked.

I just can't believe how respectful all the kids, and the whole high school rodeo association have been toward our feelings, and how they all continue to honor Michael's memory in such wonderful ways. I am so proud that he had such good friends through rodeo.

The stickers that were made that said *In Memory of Michael Glynn*, with a cross and a bull rider on them, were everywhere. Kids not only had them on their riding vests, but on their rope bags, trailers and pickups.

I am in awe of everyone. I will never be able to thank everyone enough, or properly, for what they have given us–these beautiful tributes and memories of Michael.

You have all inspired me to be a better person. I am forever grateful to have you in my life, and to know that you were in Michael's. God bless you all.

Tuesday, June 27, 2006

Dear Michael,

I look at your picture almost constantly. I think about you constantly. I will love and remember you forever.

The first of your goals this year was not able to be met. You went to Heaven before you were able to compete in the high school rodeos. The boys that are state champions, and those going to nationals are very deserving. I wonder how you would have done in the arena this year.

Would you have rode perfectly, scored high and met your goal? Or would you have bucked off? Or worse, would you have gotten hurt?

Would you have had a glorious and successful summer of bull riding? Or would you have been hurt and unable to rodeo or work?

Would you have been anxious to move to Chadron for college? Or would you have changed your mind at the last minute and decided to not go?

Would you have graduated from college and come home to run our ranch? Or would you have ended up working at a fast food place?

Would you have met and married the love of your life and given us lots of grandchildren to cherish? Or would you have stayed single, or gotten divorced?

Would you have known children, grandchildren and even great-grandchildren? Or would you have suffered at the loss of someone you loved?

Would you have been happy through your golden years, playing with your own grandchildren? Or would you have been lonely, unhappy and miserable to be close to?

These are all questions that haunt my mind daily, questions that will never be answered. Life on earth is beautiful. But life here can also have times of sadness and disappointment. Your eighteen years here were filled with both. You brought insurmountable joy to my life, and your death brought insurmountable pain to my life. I feel like a puzzle that is missing a piece.

Even though I still have your brother and sister, I am no longer complete. I think I should be angry with you for recklessly drinking and driving, and speeding, which caused the accident that took your life on earth away. But I can't. My heart is too full of love for you. I just can't be angry.

I want you back here with me. But I know you're where God wants you – where he wants all of us to be at the right time. Life here is full of beauty – you were proof of that. I can only imagine how beautiful your life is now in Heaven.

I try to tell myself that one day I'll feel better, and that this emptiness will be filled with something. But no one, and no thing, could ever take your place. I will try to feel better, for everyone else, but I know I never will.

I have to at least begin to accept the fact that you're gone. Only with the Grace of God can that happen.

Although your friends and my friends have been wonderful and helpful, it is God alone that will get me through the rest of my life without you.

Just know, kiddo, that I will always be grateful to God for letting me have you as long as I did. You were one of the three most precious gifts I have ever been given.

I thank God for you, always.

And I thank God that you are now forever safe, with Him, and will never have to live with the sadness I am feeling from losing you.

Hugs and kisses always,
Mom

Wednesday, June 28, 2006

I left work early today. We had an appointment with an agent about Michael's life insurance policy. We bought policies for each of our kids when they were around two years old. It was meant to be an investment for them for college. We wanted to have it build a cash value that we could borrow against to help pay some college expenses. We borrowed against one of Roger's policies when we bought the ranch from his parents, and it was a good move financially. Life insurance for young children is very inexpensive, and we also planned it so our kids would have some when they started out with a family, without having to pay larger premiums then. I don't think anyone ever buys life insurance thinking they'll actually have to use the death benefit. But here we are, getting a check from the company. It was by no means a lot, but it will cover most of the funeral expenses. I also got some college financial aid papers for Michael in the mail today. This is what we should be doing - finalizing loans and payments for college this fall. But I'm paying his funeral expenses instead.

We had a good visit with the insurance agent. We shared a lot of stories about Michael with him. We even caught ourselves laughing a lot as we reminisced. Sometimes I feel guilty about laughing and thinking about anything other than Michael. Amber told me today she feels the same way. I told her that I know God wants us to start doing some of our "regular" things in life. After all, our life is still going on. I also told her that the more often we realize for a moment that we haven't thought about Michael because we were doing anything else, or enjoying something, it means that we are moving forward and continuing to live our life. I don't think God wants us to feel guilty about being happy about something. And there are so very many things in life to be happy about. I think that's what makes me feel the saddest, really. I see all these wonderful things in the world, and I wish so much that Michael could be experiencing them also. It breaks my heart that he can't, and won't be able to.

I need to have Michael here with me. God is slowly and lovingly shaking me and saying that it is not going to happen.

How do people get through losing a child, or any loved one for that matter, without God in their lives? I'm having a hard enough time of it the way it is. I don't even want to imagine doing this without God by my side.

I pray tonight that everyone else saddened by Michael's death has asked God to be with them also.

Thursday, June 29, 2006

Today was one of those days that everything just seemed to go pretty well. There were only a couple of times that I felt shaky and quivery. I know, those are kind of odd descriptive words. But sometimes lately my hands just start shaking, for no apparent reason. That's not especially good when I spend so much time typing! And I feel like my voice gets "quivery" when I talk. My throat gets tight and I can actually feel it vibrating. Then there are the headaches. Those happen a lot anymore. But, all in all, today was okay.

A good friend of Michael's left today for California for a couple of weeks. Before she left we were talking about driving down the road and hearing certain songs that made us think of Michael. We discovered that there's one we both can't help but smile and laugh about now. It's Brad Paisley's song called *The World*.

One day this spring when the boys and I were on our way to town for school and work, Michael looked out the window and said, very slowly and thoughtfully, "to the world you may be just another girl, but to me, baby, you are the world."

I kind of went nuts! (I had never heard the song on the radio as of yet). I excitedly asked Michael if he had made that up, and he said something flip like, "well, gee, what do you think." I later realized that he didn't exactly tell me "yes" but he hadn't exactly said "no" either. You had to be cautious with how you asked Michael things. He was good at getting off on technicalities.

Anyway, I told Michael he better write down what he just said so he wouldn't forget it, because I thought it was a wonderful and catchy phrase. I actually told him he should try to sell it to Hallmark for a greeting card! He just said with a sly grin, "Ya think so?"

Well, pretty soon we were in town and I dropped the kids off and went to work, not thinking much about his clever little ditty again – until about a week later, when we were going home one night, and there it was on the radio. I was dumbfounded. Michael just laughed and laughed at me. I could be so gullible to his jokes and antics. The lyrics to that song are proof.

For the first few days after Michael died, when I heard that song I would start to cry. Now, I hear it and it makes me smile. I can still have tears, but I also have a happy, silly memory to go with them. I think when this happens, I'm in a good place to be.

I pray that all of you can find smiles to go along with your tears when you have memories of Michael.

I'm going to close tonight with my opinion of the new underage drinking and driving law about to take effect. Legislators think they're doing a good thing by making the law more consistent with what adults get for a sentence/fine if they are arrested for a DUI. Instead of lessening the MIC punishment for kids, why don't they increase the DUI punishment for adults? With all of the people who are killed by drunken drivers, or who die in their own drinking/driving accident, it would seem to me that as far as punishment, more would be better.

Friday, June 30, 2006

The weirdest thing just happened. And I mean JUST happened. I was sitting here reading some e-mail messages. Matt is in here with me watching tv – some redneck show on CMT. Roger got up from the living room to come in the kitchen and get a drink, and I asked him if he was ready to call it a night and go to bed. I just barely caught myself, and almost said, "I'll stay up and wait for Michael to get home." The last couple of days have seemed very normal for me. And saying that tonight would have been a normal thing to say on a Friday night at 10:30 p.m. Thankfully, I caught myself and didn't say it out loud. But it just felt so weird to still think it, and almost say it.

Really, though, the last couple of days have gone well, considering. I think it's because I've kept myself busy at work. At first I really, really wanted to quit my job. I had no desire to work, and I still struggle with a desire to write news for the paper. But people said I shouldn't quit, and I guess they were right. I'm actually going to write a news article for the paper next week - something other than the editorial column I've taken up. I think it will be good for me. And I've got the whole weekend to get it done. It might just take me that long!

I feel like I consume these journal entries with feelings about myself, and leave out the rest of my family. I don't mean to. I am very concerned about everyone else. Sometimes I just don't know what to do for them to help them get through this, when I don't know what to do for myself. How can I help somebody else, when I'm such a mess? Roger and I talk about things sometimes. Sometimes we really disagree about things dealing with Michael's death. He gets bent out of shape if he opens a hospital bill that the insurance company hasn't paid yet. And I just have an "oh, well" attitude about those kind of things now.

I think if someone came to me right now and said I'd feel better, and feel like I hadn't let Michael down as a mother if I would give everything I had to them, I'd do it. Someone very dear to me said today that their kids have in the past, and sometimes even now, think of her as a #$%@&. I can sure relate to that. Michael used to think, at least sometimes, I hope not always – that I was the biggest #$%@& in the world. I pray so, so hard that he didn't die hating me. I used to tell my kids, when they were a little younger, that I didn't always like what they had done, but that I always loved them. I hope Michael, although he may have thought I was a #$%@&, still loved me.

I don't know if Roger feels any of these same things or not. He doesn't say, and doesn't seem to want to talk about it. So I guess it's just me. The same goes for Matt. I don't think I've heard him say Michael's name more than a handful of times since his death. I wish we could all sit down together and talk, but I know I can't force them to until they're ready. And maybe they never will. Amber and I talk quite often about Michael. Like she said, it's amazing how they used to fight like cats and dogs when they were little, yet virtually every memory she has as a child involves Michael, including all her good memories.

I know Mikey's not going to come home tonight. But I think I'll stay up a little while longer anyway. It just seems like a normal thing to do.

God bless us all.

Chapter 3

Saturday, July 1, 2006

I had no "uumph" today. Surprise, surprise. I was really looking forward to this weekend because we had no plans to go anywhere! I was hoping to get lots of things done at home, but that's kind of gone by the wayside. Maybe it was a good day to just soak in resting.

I've been looking at Michael's pictures a lot. Now I realize just why they make me feel like it's not real, and he's still here, somewhere. I have taken most of the pictures. In all the years we've been married, I don't think Roger has taken a dozen pictures of the kids, or anything at all. So, I was the one who was talking to Michael, saying, "say cheese" and so forth. He was looking at the camera, but he was also looking at me because I was right behind the camera. The senior pictures- I especially feel strange looking at them.

I had been hounding Michael for weeks to get these taken. He wanted to go to a professional photographer for senior pictures. I told him I had the paper's camera I could use, which is very, very nice, and they could be printed on their professional printer. Michael argued for weeks with me. I finally got Roger's support to help me, and we spent the afternoon of Roger's birthday, April 15, taking Michael's senior pictures, at home. I was so excited about it.

We went down to our corrals in our timber area, which is very rustic, and "Michael." I had a blast. Roger was driving, and when I'd see a setting I liked I would make him stop and I'd pile out and drag Michael out with me. Of course he complained the whole time, but I think it was kind of a good-natured complaining. He just thought I was taking too many, and it was taking too long. (We were finished in about an hour). Michael was always so photogenic, and I was having so much fun. I would tell him where to stand, or he would tell me where he was going to stand. I would try to make jokes and get him to smile. He would grumble and say, "just take the #$%@& picture!" Then just before I snapped, he would smile just right. He was having fun, and I knew it. He just wanted to give me grief.

A couple of days later he went to Martin and took some studio shots, and some at their arena chutes. He asked me if we could just say that Tim took all of his photos, and I told him that was fine with me. He thought it was embarrassing that his mom took the pictures. I think in the end, he was ok with my taking his pictures, because they turned out great! And now, I am so very glad that I was the one who took them. I look at all of them now, and I can relive the whole day – which happened exactly one month before his accident. I never thought at the time it would be one of the last family experiences we would have with him. It makes me cherish all of the other things we did together the past 18 years. And it makes me want to not miss one single moment of the future with Matt before he's out of school and gone.

Sunday, July 2, 2006

With all the talking and thinking I did yesterday about Michael's pictures, today I took the huge pile of them that were on the dining table, and put them in his bedroom. I just moved the pile, literally, on to his bed. I'll sort them out later and put some more in frames, or something. I want to leave them on his bed, to deter me from sleeping in there. I haven't for almost a week now. The last two times I did, I had really bad nightmares, and left the room scared. The room is at a point that it's very hard to be in there now. Most of his things are in boxes, but there are still a lot of pictures on the walls and the dressers, and all his shirts are still in the closet.

I went through the shirts today and remembered when and where he got each one. I know which ones he liked the best, and the ones he hardly ever wore. He was very picky about his closet. All his t-shirts had to be on the left side, and the long-sleeved western shirts on the right. They all had to be facing toward the middle. His coats were on the side of the western shirts, between the ones he wore for everyday and the ones he wore for good and at rodeos. The rest of his room could be an absolute disaster area, but his closet had to be just right! I can't imagine ever getting rid of his shirts. He was proud of them, and took a lot of care deciding which one to wear. At one time I thought of making them into a quilt, which would still be a really good idea. But I don't think I can do that for quite a while. I just can't bear the thought of cutting any of them up right now.

Roger went to Pierre today to get some things for the boat so they can take it fishing someplace other than just the little dams around here, which are drying up very quickly this summer. Matt went to Wood to seine minnows with a friend, and I was all alone for the day. It actually felt really good. It gave me the opportunity to spend the time in Michael's room, as strange as it sounds, with his shirts. When I touched them, I could feel his skin. When I looked at certain pictures, and saw that shirt in the closet, I could relive where we were, or what we were doing.

The one thing I haven't done yet, and I want to, but I'm afraid to – is get out the old home videos. I want to start watching them when I'm alone, with no chance of someone walking in and interrupting. Today would have been a good time to. But I'm just kind of scared to. I'm scared I'll just completely lose it and go crazy when I see them again. I guess, they're here in a cupboard, and safe, and waiting for me when I'm ready.

Philippians 4:6 - "Pray about everything; then, leave the outcomes up to Me. Do not fear My will, for through it I accomplish what is best for you. Take a deep breath and dive into the depths of absolute trust in Me."

Monday, July 3, 2006

Sometimes when I go to the cemetery, well, actually every time – I sit there and talk to Michael. The *Jesus Calling* book that I've become rather addicted to reminds us to spend a time of solitude each day, just praying. Today when I went to the cemetery I spent a lot of time sitting and praying. I think that's going to become a very special place of solitude for me. When I got there I immediately started crying. It is just so hard to have to realize that this is really real! But then I started praying, and it really did calm me. When I finished, I started thinking of where Michael really is now, and focusing on that, rather than where he isn't at now.

I've heard that God forgives you much sooner than you forgive yourself. That's what I'm praying for now. I need to be able to forgive myself for not doing something to prevent the accident that took Michael's life. In time, it may happen.

Tuesday, July 4, 2006

Independence Day is today. Roger and Matt went to Valentine and took my nephew fishing. I'll probably go down later this evening and watch fireworks with everyone. It's way too dry and dangerous here for fireworks. I'd kind of like to just spend the rest of the day and evening alone too.

I keep thinking about it being Independence Day, and about our state's laws. That always brings me back to the people that buy alcohol for minors, and of course then the one that bought for Michael and the seniors this year. This is America, the land of the free. But why do people who buy for minors get all the breaks of "being free." I know, their true justice will be served on Judgment Day. But until then, do we have to just sit around on earth and ignore what they are doing to our kids? My God, Michael is dead!

And how many other kids are dead because someone bought alcohol for them? God has given us the intelligence to initiate a justice system here in America, so why isn't it used? If we continue to just ignore, and ignore, and ignore these crimes, more and more kids will grow up to either become alcoholics, or buy alcohol themselves for minors who could die in accidents. They'll know they can get away with it, because we let them.

Thank God, Michael is freer now than any of us. He is free of sin, sorrow and sadness, living with Our Savior Christ in Heaven. That is comforting to know. But even knowing that is not enough to take away my constant pain!

If any of you have ever bought alcohol for minors, please stop. If any of you kids drink alcohol, please stop. It is just not worth it! Please, take it from me. I really do know what I'm talking about! This is like living in a hell on earth. Knowing that you have to get up and face every single day for the rest of your life without the possibility of seeing your child, ever, is agonizing. Actually, there isn't even a word to adequately describe it.

I don't know if it makes any difference how your child dies. No matter what, it's got to be like this. But to know that the whole accident was because Michael was so intoxicated that he couldn't focus on driving, well, again there are no words. It just gives me a very sick feeling all over.

If no one would have agreed to sell those kids alcohol, Michael would be alive today. I know it, and so does everyone else. So why is are those who did, still able to be out there, buying alcohol for more kids? How many dead teenagers do they want on his conscious? Or do they have a conscious?

Thursday, July 6, 2006

Last night we went to the last of Matt's summer league basketball games. His team won the championship! We didn't stay to watch the championship game for the other home team. Matt had to be on a horse by 6 a.m. this morning, and it was getting late. We didn't get home until midnight the way it was.

As I sat at the game, I thought of Michael so much. And that was so odd. Michael only played basketball during middle school. He wasn't a bad player, but he just didn't like to play the game. He shot hoops at home with Matt and Roger all the time, and he always went to the games, but he didn't like to play at school. Matt is just the opposite. He loves basketball, and any sport actually. Michael's passion was rodeo, and in school it was football.

In all the basketball games I've been to watching Matt, I hardly ever thought about Mike. If I did, it was to wonder where he was, or how he was getting home, or some trivial thing like that. Yet, as I sat in that gym and cheered for Matt and his team, my thoughts continually drifted towards Mike.

Why do I think of him all the time now that he's gone, in places I hardly ever thought of him when he was alive? Will it always be like this? I feel when it happens that I would just love for a little bit, to get him out of my mind, so I could really concentrate on something else. But I can't. Then I feel guilty for having thought that. I mean, what kind of a mother would actually want to not think of her dead child?

Dead child. What awful words those are. When you look at them in writing like this, it's so different than hearing or saying them. The two words should not be allowed to exist together.

A portion of today's Bible reading says "Ask My Spirit to calm your mind, for He and I work in perfect harmony. Be still and attentive in My Presence. You are on holy ground." Those are definitely words to live by.

Thursday, July 6, 2006

Tonight we watched the SD High School Finals Short Go on PBS. Last year at the finals rodeo, Michael rode every single bull he got on. In the first round he got a re-ride, and rode. And on Saturday he rode a bull that they told us later they didn't expect anyone to be able to ride. He was a dirty little bull that turned, jumped and bucked, all at once. Of course, we thought Michael should have gotten more points. Parents always do! But he did well. In the short go, he rode, but it was the sloppiest ride of the whole weekend! And that's the one that everyone saw later on TV! He was so mad at that! People, especially "city folks" told him he looked great, but he knew it was just plain sloppy and they were either being nice, or didn't know a good ride from a bad one.

He ended up third in the finals average, but missed the national team by one point last year. He couldn't wait for regions this year, and just knew he was going to make it on the national team.

We were in Belle Fourche for the second round and the short go this year, but yet we weren't really there. So it was nice to watch it tonight on TV. Mikey might have made it to nationals, but the kids who did make it really rode well. They truly deserve to go. He would have been proud of all of them. One rider said during an interview that bull riders don't really compete against each other, but against the bull. I don't know how many times Michael said that very same thing!!! He wanted all of his "buds" to do well. He just always wanted to draw a bull that was better than their draw.

We were also able to notice tonight on TV, very clearly, the In Memory of Michael Glynn sticker that most of the riders had on their vests. He may not have been there in body, but he was definitely there in spirit. It was very nice to see that he was a part of so many of those riders – his friends, during the rodeos.

Today I was told that the Northern Bull Riding Tour scheduled for White River this year is going to be dedicated to the Memory of Michael Glynn. They're going to say something about it at the beginning, and give a memorial plaque to the winner. Michael loved the NBRT. He rode their junior bulls each year, and just as soon as he was old enough, paid his membership and rode with the big boys. He consistently went to their bull ridings last summer, and made it to the finals last fall. The finals were the same night as a football game in Philip. He chose to go the finals, thinking there were still four football games he could play in.

Well, he got his knee stepped on in the first go Friday night but rode, and also rode in the second go. He was qualified then for the short go on Saturday. We had gone to the football game to watch Matt play. He called us while we were on our way home and told us how he did. Man, was he excited! He was on his way to winning the saddle, and he sure wanted it! We were planning to go watch him on Saturday. He told us he got stepped on, but really downplayed it. He spent the night at Amber's house (in Sioux Falls, where the finals are held), and the next morning she called us and said she had taken him to the emergency room. He couldn't even walk. He was going to try to ride that night, but we decided not to go, because we didn't think he would. And he didn't. He couldn't even get out of bed.

We went to Winner the next day to meet him and pick him up. As soon as we saw him, we took him straight to the hospital in Pierre. He had a temperature of 104, was nauseas, and could hardly move. They did surgery on his knee the next morning and removed a portion of the meniscus lining. But then, he got an infection in it, and ended up in the hospital for a whole week! Even after he got home, he couldn't get around to go to school for another week.

So – he missed the rest of his senior football season. The day I brought him home from the hospital he said, "I kind of wish I'd have just gone to the football game." Then he looked over again and said, "but riding those bulls was sure fun!" Mikey was completely addicted to riding bulls.

Friday, July 7, 2006

Things are getting kind of scary at home. And that's just because of the weather. When I came down our road this evening after work, I noticed a huge amount of black smoke just to the west of us. Our neighbor saw it too and was in her driveway calling other neighbors. We called the fire department, who was already on their way out. You couldn't even see the smoke from our house, though. We live in a real low spot, with a hill on all sides. The fire was actually north of Corn Creek, and had apparently been started by some local kids over there. It was stopped by the road, and didn't look like it burned a lot of ground, but got into some trees and bushes, which made the smoke and smoldering last a long time. We were told there were six fires in the county tonight. Some were caused by lightning from a storm that came through – in the eastern and southern parts. We didn't even get a drop on our place.

The first time Roger let Michael go with him to fight a fire, was when he was about 10 or 12 years old. It was a grass fire in our far north pasture. Michael felt so grown-up. I guess out here, it's like a rite of passage to becoming a man.

Michael may not have had the opportunity to live to be an old man, but I'm very grateful, having grown up in a town, that he, and all my kids, were able to be country kids. Whether it's riding a horse before they could walk, or learning how to fight a prairie fire, it's a great way of life for kids.

But, here goes my soapbox again. The dangers of drinking and driving were more than even a tough country kid could overcome.

God Bless, and pray for rain.

Sunday, July 9, 2006

Now I know why it's a good thing to get back to work. I'm so busy during the week that my mind doesn't wander as easily. These weekends, though – they just suck. I have absolutely no desire to do anything at home.

We shouldn't be here, and it really bothers me. And to make matters worse, the weather has made it very depressing at home. We should be spending our weekends watching Michael ride, like we've done for so very many years. But we're not. We sit at home. Bored. Bored - with laundry, dishes and dust piling high. And I just don't care.

Then there's the weather. Everything, and I mean everything, is bone dry here. There is nothing green, except the leaves on some trees and the weeds that have surfaced. Roger said that in our north summer pasture, he thinks the cows are now breaking off more grass than they're eating. It is so brittle. There have been fires every day in the county. I think everyone is on pins and needles knowing another is to be expected.

I slept in Michael's bed last night. I just couldn't help it. I couldn't sleep, so I ventured in. Roger must be spending some time in the room, too, because things weren't as I last left them. I've always had the closet door open wide, so I could look at his shirts, and dream of him being in them. But the door was shut tight. His gear bag was on the opposite side of the closet floor, and a box of his pictures and things was now in that place. Regardless, I fell asleep quickly, and slept well.

It's been almost two months now, and I still haven't changed or even washed the bedding in Michael's room. I don't even have the bedspread actually spread over the bed. It just gets crumpled and bundled up on top, until I go in and curl up in it the next time. I'm so afraid of losing what is left of his smell that is in there. I'd rather have it dirty, than lose the scent of Michael.

Yesterday, when Roger came in for lunch, I told him I had accomplished one thing so far. I wrote letters to the recipients of Michael's organs. There is a process we have to use, and we actually send the letters to Life Source, and they make sure we haven't given out any private information that we're not allowed to yet, then forward them to the recipient. Roger told me the day Michael died that someday I would want to know more about the organ recipients. I didn't believe him. But he was right.

More than anything, I want to know that those people are still alive. As long as they're alive, so is something of Michael's. If they die, will I mourn again, or more? I know the organs are just a piece of his body, and not his soul or spirit, which was the real Michael. But on the other hand – they were a piece of his body. They were part of my and Roger's flesh and blood. Did we do the right thing? Could we handle any more loss? Do I really want to know? I guess I'll go ahead and send them, because not knowing is harder right now. I keep telling myself that Michael didn't have to die to save other lives; it was because he had already died, that other lives were saved. But saying things, and believing them, right now at least, can be two completely different things.

Soon – this endless weekend will be over.

Sunday, July 9, 2006

Michael committed a crime. He drove a vehicle after he'd been drinking. He should have been stopped by the police. He should have either been sent to jail to spend the night, and/or he should have had a fine to pay. But that didn't happen. He paid the price for his crime though. He died.

He died.

He died.

He died.

Maybe if I see it often enough, it will seem real.

I would like to pay for his crime. I'll pay a fine. I'll go to jail. I'll do community service. It doesn't matter. Nothing could be more than the price of not having my son to ever touch, hold or talk to again.

But the other crime that night – the one where someone supplied my son and a whole bunch of other young kids with alcohol – what's happening there? It eats away at me daily, like a cancer.

Why should some pay for their crimes, and others don't? I want someone to take Michael's death seriously! I want someone to take the cause of it seriously! I want someone to do something about it!

Michael is dead.

Michael is dead.

Michael is dead.

Michael is dead.

Will someone please notice???

Monday, July 10, 2006

Today was by far one of the worst days I've had in a while. I thought yesterday was bad, but today topped it. There was almost nothing that didn't make me cry. It started when someone, unknowing how I would take it, told me that more needs to be done to get parents to stop their kids from drinking. She said "it starts in the home" and went on talking about how parents can't let their kids drink, or more of these things are going to happen. The thing is – I've been feeling so guilty about Michael's death, and motherhood in general. It's been extremely hard not to blame myself completely for Michael's accident. I think I always will, even though people are nice enough to tell me not to. The most important job a mother can have is to protect her child, and I failed. I guess, now that I think about it, this person today was probably being more honest with me than anyone has. It's just not easy to hear. Maybe the reason it's so hard to hear, is because I know it's true. Anyway, from then on the day just went downhill.

When I finally got home tonight, there was a package for us. It was from Life Source. It was a beautiful certificate and a letter explaining the situation of each of the recipients of Michael's organs.

The man who received his heart was moved to the top of the transplant waiting list in April. The letter gave a few more specifics about each of the individuals, such as how long they had been on the donor list, what their specific diseases were, whether they were married or single, and had children. A lady who received one of Michael's lungs, has since passed away. I cried. It's like another piece of Michael died – again.

Now I don't know how much more I want to know about these people. When they die (as we all will someday), will I feel another loss? I know it won't be exactly the same as with Michael, but there is still a part of him in them, and I think I might feel with the others like I did tonight about the lady who died. Today was just a rotten day. I shouldn't dwell on my self-loathing, or grieve for the "lady with the lung" who died. Seven other people are still alive! Thank God.

Tuesday, July 11, 2006

On the roller coaster of my life, I headed uphill today. Actually, it wasn't that hard to do. From yesterday, almost every direction is up! I have to say, without the grace of God and the caring words of good friends, I would never even want to come up from the down days.

A friend's comment on my journal yesterday really hit home with me tonight. Yes, Michael danced. Of course, when I first read it, as usual I cried – almost uncontrollably. What a beautiful thing to say. And what truth! Thank God Michael danced his way through life. And he did it not knowing when his last day would be, just as none of us know our own time to leave this earth.

A lot of cards I read say things like 'just know that the sun will come up tomorrow' and similar sentiments. Some days I think 'what a stupid thing to say.' I mean, we don't know that the sun will come up tomorrow. Yet we expect it to. And do we always get up in the morning and thank God for something as simple as letting the sun come up?

I think I used to take for granted that the sun would be coming up. I know now that it really might not. It didn't for Michael. If something should happen, and the sun didn't come up for me tomorrow, I would want to know that I spent my life dancing. Is it possible to feel bad, sad and desperate when you're dancing, literally? I never have.

So, I'm going to try my hardest to dance every day of the rest of my life. I want to spend my life dancing, not feeling sorry for myself. And I'm going to thank God for each rising sun. God is good, all the time! All the time, God is good!

Wednesday, July 12, 2006
Thank God, the sun came up this morning. And God willing, it will tomorrow, too.

I have to share with you a positive step Matt took last week, at least it seemed positive to me. He started riding in Mike's saddle. It may not seem like that big of a deal, but in our family it is. Roger's brother Cliff, was a rodeo fanatic, like Michael. Cliff rode bulls, saddle broncs, dogged and roped. He was killed in a car accident when he was 19, while he was at a pro rodeo in New Mexico. He was changing the tire on his car, when another ran into him, and took off. He had won an all-around saddle at a Little Britches rodeo in Chadron, Nebraska when he was in high school. After he died, it sat in our barn for all these years. When I came into the family and heard the story, I really thought the saddle should be preserved better. But it seemed like, even all those years later, no one here wanted to really deal with it. So it sat there. When Michael was about 14 years old, he asked Roger if he could ride Cliff's saddle. Of course, Roger let him. I think Roger was very honored that Michael thought so much of an uncle he never knew, and just riding in that saddle made the connection even stronger. Roger even let Michael use Cliff's old bull rope a couple of times, but it was a grass rope and not very good or safe, so it didn't happen too often. A couple of years later, Roger's other brother, Clayton, brought his saddle back to the ranch and gave it to Michael. It's the one Michael has used mostly since. And it's the one that Matt has now started riding in.

Sometimes when I feel really low, I can't imagine how Roger feels, losing an 18 year old son, when he has also gone through losing a 19 year old brother – especially when Cliff and Mikey were apparently so very much alike. It does break my heart.

I asked Roger last night if he can remember Cliff's voice. He said he still kind of does. I've been thinking about Michael's voice lately. I remember specific things he used to say to me all the time, and I play them over and over in my head, trying to make sure I always remember his voice. Thank God we have video tapes.

Thursday, July 13, 2006
On my way out of White River today, I had to stop at the cemetery and talk to Michael. I couldn't believe the cross and his gravesite. It is just so beautiful. The eagle feathers a friend put there are such an incredible honor. It's rather overwhelming to see. Someone put their graduation tassle on the cross a couple of weeks ago, and now a graduation sash is on there, too. There are also a couple more cross necklaces adorning the old wooden cross. It's just so beautiful. I sure hope Michael knew when he was alive just how much he meant to everyone. He always joked around and said that he was "the next big deal." But I hope he truly understood how much he meant to people. Personally, I don't think he did. I guess he's proof, now, that we need to show or tell those we love, that we do love them, each and every day. You never know when you won't get the chance again.

God's blessing to you all.

Monday, July 17, 2006
At home tonight, there was the most beautiful letter in the mail. It came from Life Source, and enclosed was a letter from the man who received Michael's heart. The letter was just perfect. He said all the right things, and is especially grateful. He is in his 40's, married, and has four children. He talked about how his life has completely changed, and that he thinks of our son every single day. Reading the letter made me truly realize that Roger is right - I wouldn't mind getting to know the donor recipients.

Tuesday, July 18, 2006
I look at pictures of Michael all the time. They're all over our house. They're on my computers. They're in my office at work. It has made it feel like he's not really gone, that he's still here. I mean, he's looking right at me!

How can he really be gone? How can somebody just be erased from the earth so quickly? I know - I have many memories, and of course, all these pictures. But it's just not the same, obviously.

How can these things happen?

We live in such a fast-paced world. Even here in the boonies, we expect things to happen quickly. We never have enough time to do things. Maybe that's why I just can't imagine having to wait, and wait, and wait, to someday see Michael again.

Why is it possible to protect your children from colds and sniffles, sharp corners on furniture, rattlesnakes and waspy cows, then in the blink of an eye you can't do anything to help them. And then they're gone. Forever. There are no do-overs.

Please, please, please - I am begging all of the other kids out there who are reading this - don't put yourself in harm's way. For the sake of all the mothers of the world who may have to live without their child, please make wise choices!

God's blessings to everyone.

Wednesday, July 19, 2006

I think I've just about resigned myself to the realization that nothing is going to be done to the people who bought the alcohol for the seniors this year at their fateful graduation party. I don't think the right people care. Actually, I don't think Michael was the "right" kind of person. Oh how I wish these people would be punished to the point that they would quit contributing to the harm of our kids. One person in our town actually told me the other day that if one particular person hadn't bought the kids their beer, six others would have been in line to. Does that make it okay? I guess in her mind it does, but it sure doesn't in mine. Again - punish them and they might quit. How can people live with themselves with this kind of an attitude? I don't understand, and I'm actually kind of glad I don't understand. I don't want to be the kind of person that understands that kind of mentality.

I'd still like to have one last talk with the authorities. I'm pretty sure it won't do any good. I know nothing will bring Michael back, but what if it could end up saving someone else some day?

What really is the point of having laws if people don't abide by them, and we don't stand together and make our elected officials prosecute those who break them?

I'd really like to keep up the fight this time, but I'm so tired. I don't feel like I'm getting anywhere, and I don't feel like I have enough support.

I wonder how many people think Michael got what he deserved for drinking and driving. I'm not so naive to think that everyone loved him. I also know that although some people are now saying how wonderful he was, they thought when he was alive that he was a 'wild little #$%& ', and probably not a good influence on their own kids. I've kind of wondered lately if that isn't part of the reason nothing is being done to the person who admitted to the police that he bought for the kids that night. Yes, he admitted he did, and is probably still out there buying for others kids all the time. Why is he so special, and above the law? Was my child really that bad of a kid? Doesn't Michael's death from the alcohol that someone else provided to him mean anything?

I guess not.

Please, God, protect and watch over all of us as we journey through this sorry-state-of-society that we have created.

Thursday, July 20, 2006

I get this feeling that some people are thinking that I'm going overboard with this "I'm never going to drink again" and "someone needs to be punished for Michael's death" attitude I've got.

Well, I think it's getting obvious that some kids, and adults, are forgetting that Michael is dead. And that he died at the hands of alcohol. Alcohol. I used to think "just what will it take to make people understand the negative effects it has on our kids?" Then Michael died. Yes, Michael chose to drink. And Michael chose to get in that car and drive. Did Michael choose to have an accident that would take his life? No. It happened, including him getting into that car to drive, because alcohol does not make you think straight. It alters your brain cells! That is "Alcohol Ed 101" at it's simplest.

Some people may have forgotten that Michael is dead. Some people may have forgotten just what led to his death. Some people may forget about him a year from now. Some people may forget about him ten years from now. But I will never forget. I could be a 95 year old woman with alzheimers disease, and I won't forget!

I will never drink even a sip of any alcohol again. I don't care. It's just not necessary. I have nothing to prove to people - like "I'm cool" or "one little drink won't hurt me" and I now have a whole new incredible respect for others who don't drink - even a little.

I'm doing this because of Michael. Those who choose to not drink, that aren't doing it because of Michael, well, you are my heroes. You have real courage. God bless you all.

Friday, July 21, 2006

I went to the cemetery after work to put some flowers on Michael's grave. With the bull-riding coming up in White River tomorrow night, I just thought he should have an extra bunch of flowers. Silly, isn't it. Seeing his name on the cross makes it seem real that he's gone. Yet, seeing his name on the cross doesn't seem real. It's very confusing.

When I went to leave, I got in the car, turned it on, and the radio immediately started playing the Gary Allen song *Life Ain't Always Beautiful*. I just sat there through the whole thing, listening and staring at Michael's name on the cross. It was almost like Michael was talking to me – singing the words in the song. When the song was over, the DJ said, White River loves it's country (they say that a lot, just substituting different towns – this exact time they said 'White River').

So, was this a sign – from Michael? Do I even believe in signs? I'm not sure. I think I do. But I don't want to dwell on looking for them. So, was this a coincidence? I don't believe in coincidences. It's very confusing.

But, you know what? It made me feel good. It made me feel very good. Any day that happens, is a good day.

Life ain't always beautiful – but it's a beautiful ride.

Michael had a short life, but he made it a beautiful ride – for himself and all of us who loved him so much!

God's blessings.

Saturday, July 22, 2006

I'm writing today's entry a little early today. Can't seem to get any housework done anyway. We'll be at the White River bull-o-rama tonight. They're going to do a tribute to Michael, and I've been trying to write something about him for it. They asked me to weeks ago, and as usual, I'm putting it off until the day it's due!

I started out (and will probably leave it) writing about how much he loved bull riding, and his awards and accomplishments in the sport. But then I started remembering how bad he was at it sometimes!

I remember one summer when we went to 14 rodeos in a row and Michael bucked off every single time! I was getting frustrated. He was still young enough that I drove him to most all of them. We were on the road constantly. We'd get to a 4-h or Little Britches rodeo to check in by 8:00 or 9:00 a.m. then sit around all day.

Anyway, bull riding was almost always the very last event. Finally, by 6, 7 or even 8:00 p.m., he would be up to ride. We had been there for 10 hours or more, just to watch an 8-second ride, and he would buck off, or fall off, in four or five seconds. And this happened 14 times in a row!

On the way home after Buck Off #14, I made him an offer. He wanted a brand new Dodge pickup so badly, with all the bells and whistles. I told him that if he could ride 20 bulls in a row, in competition, I would buy him a Dodge pickup. He didn't trust that I would actually do it, so when we got home he wrote up a contract on a piece of scratch paper and brought it to me to sign. I did. He pinned it to the bulletin board in his room. He was so excited and told everyone he was going to do it.

Of course, I didn't tell him I would be buying him the precise Dodge pickup he wanted, and I didn't say I would be buying him a brand new one. When we got that clarified, he was a little disappointed. But I told him I really would get him a pickup.

Know what? He rode the very next bull he got on! I think he rode about 9 bulls in a row (I was getting a little nervous by then). When he finally bucked off, and the Dodge pickup contract was voided, he was only a little disappointed. By then he had realized what I was really trying to give him. He had gotten his confidence back.

Bucking off a lot of times in a row can wear you down. He needed to have something in his sight to be riding for. At that point in his life, he wanted a pickup more than anything else, and he was working towards that goal. He missed that goal, but found others along the way, the most important – feeling good about himself and his ability again.

We did buy him a pickup eventually– a green Ford that he and Roger picked out. And it was definitely a used one!

I have so many memories like this of Michael, and of all my kids. You try so hard to teach them right from wrong, to fulfill their needs, to help them become good people, to fix their problems and give them another chance – sometimes doing things you don't agree with or believe in, just to try to protect them, to love them unconditionally; then you let them out of your sight for what seems like a split second, and the monsters of the world attack them, and they're gone. And we're left with nothing more than memories. It's just not right.

Then someone says – alcohol itself isn't that bad if you know how to control it.

I say to them - walk in my shoes for one minute. I absolutely, without a doubt, guarantee that you will feel differently.

Once again, it's time to "head to the rodeo." Once again, we're not going to watch Michael, but to hear an announcer read a tribute to him. It's just not right.

Ephesians 5:15-18 – Be very careful, then, how you live – not as unwise but as wise, making the most of every opportunity, because the days are evil. Therefore do not be foolish, but understand what the Lord's will is. Do not get drunk on wine, which leads to debauchery. Instead, be filled with the Spirit.

God's blessings to all, through Jesus Christ!

Sunday, July 23, 2006

Today I was doing laundry. As usual, I put all the clean socks and sports shorts in a basket.

I've done this for quite a while, because as Mike and Matt got close in size, I couldn't tell which ones belonged to which boy. I'd fill the basket, then take it to them and have them sort which were theirs.

I was putting these clean clothes in a basket, when it dawned on me – this isn't necessary anymore. (Don't worry – this isn't the first time I've washed Matt's clothes in the past two months – it just made a big impact with me today).

From now on, all of these clothes will be just Matt's.

None of them belong to Michael.

Michael has no belongings.

There is no Michael.

Monday, July 24, 2006

I'm still in awe over the number of e-mails I get from people who say "thanks" for writing in this journal, and sharing my thoughts and feelings with everyone else.

I'm sorry, but I think a lot of what I write sounds kind of like "gibberish," especially when I read it a couple of weeks later. I'm also surprised, when reading past entries, how my mood can go off the charts one day, while the next day it's as if I'm comatose. I told a friend today that I just write how I feel, or what I've been thinking about that day, each night when I get home. I spend about 15 minutes writing, so it doesn't consume much of my time. It's been a tremendous help for me, to get my thoughts in writing, and I hope that it will serve as something with concrete memories of Michael, again, in writing. Part of the reason I do this, too, is because I'm more terrified than anything of forgetting something about him.

Today, it was a bottle of lotion that got to me.

Michael had really dry skin, even as a baby. He was always stealing my lotion (the unscented kind). Today when I put on some lotion, my skin felt especially dry and it conjured up that memory of Michael. All of a sudden I realized that I was never going to feel his skin again.

I remember rubbing his hand and arms while he was in the hospital. They felt so warm and soft, especially compared to they way he usually felt at home – full of grease or dirt! And I remember how he felt when I touched his body as it lay in the casket. It was so hard. But that was because of the embalming fluid, I later found out. Even in the casket, though, it felt drier than in the hospital, and more "like normal." Now if that isn't a crazy thing to think, I don't know what is.

Anyway, once today, I just closed my eyes, and rubbed my fingers across my arm. I imagined it was Michael's arm I was touching – caressing him to sleep like I did when he was a toddler. I'm not sure how long I did it – probably not long. But it really felt good. It felt like I was touching him, remembering his feel. I think that's got to be something only a mother could do. After all, he was a part of me. So if I feel myself, I can feel him – kind of.

I have pictures to remember his face and smile.

I have video tapes to remember his voice and the way he walked.

But there is nothing but my memories to remember his feel.

Tuesday, July 25, 2006
I wrote a check in a store today, and the clerk asked where Belvidere was. Our address is Belvidere, although we live in Mellette County (Belvidere is in Jackson County) and we do most of our business in White River - work and school. I was explaining this, for the umpteenth time, and it reminded me of Michael. The very simplest of things will spark these old memories.

Anyway, when he was very small, his grandpa Glynn was usually the only picked to take calves to the vet in Kadoka. We went through one year, when like most others in the area, we seemed to be hit hard with and over-eating disease in the baby calves. It seemed like grandpa and Mikey went almost every day, to either take a new calf there, or pick one up that had been there a couple of days. Grandpa would always stop in Belvidere and buy Mikey some candy. Michael couldn't say Belvidere, but called it "Bubba Dibber." To this day, we sometimes pull through Belvidere and say something like "well, we're in the big city of Bubba Dibber."

Of course, Michael very soon associated Bubba Dibber with getting candy. He loved going with grandpa on these little jaunts. He loved candy, and I hated it! Like all parents must do, I used to tell him that I couldn't wait until I was the grandparent so I could spoil his kids like his grandparents spoiled him.

Strange - what he used to think was just a cute little nickname for Belvidere, now has a different kind of meaning. We may make little jokes about it being "Bubba Dibber" but we'll have a new kind of respect when we say it - because we'll think of Michael.

There is good coming from Michael's death. We're all stronger people now. We have to be, must be, or else we wouldn't even be able to get out of bed in the morning. A stronger faith is the beginning of great things.

God's blessings - Pray for rain!

Wednesday, July 26, 2006
I went to the cemetery after work today. The eagle feathers are gone. I just can't believe that they blew off. They were on there very securely. None of the flower arrangements are gone, and they're a lot more likely to blow away than the eagle feathers were.

I know Michael's friend who put them on the cross at his grave, and I'm sure they were given with the utmost respect. That's why I'm having a hard time believing they were taken, but I also can't believe that the wind blew them off. Like I said, they were very secure.

Michael was not Native American, so maybe someone thought they shouldn't have been given to him. But that should not have been their choice. As far as I'm concerned, the only ones who had a right to remove them, was the person who put them there, or Roger and myself. And we sure didn't take them off.

I've heard stories about gravesites that have been vandalized, and family mementos that have been stolen, but I didn't think it would happen to us, or to Michael's grave. I thought anyone who would visit his grave would only do it out of respect and love. I pray that I'm not wrong. I pray that maybe the person who put the eagle feathers on the cross decided that he shouldn't have done it, and took them off himself. I would respect that.

No, Michael was not Native American. But nearly all of his closest friends were. I was very honored that his friend was so thoughtful that he gave them to Michael. But I am so very sad that they're gone.

Thursday, July 27, 2006

Matt took his sports physical today, and he's ready and anxious for football practice to start.

Michael loved football too. The only game he got to play last year was at Jones County. He made one touchdown, and was just short of catching a touchdown pass in the last seconds of the game that would have won it for White River. It was the closest White River had come to beating Jones County during Michael's high school years, and if the seniors could win just one game, they wanted it to be against their school rival.

The reason he only got to play in one game? Well, he missed the last four games of the season because of an injury at the NBRT finals. But he missed the first three games because of alcohol.

Right before Homecoming week, there was a party. Michael was there, along with almost everyone else from the high school. I can't remember now all of the details as to who found out about it, etc., but I remember asking Michael if he had been there, and he told me yes. But he also told me it was one of the few times he had gone to a party and hadn't drunk anything. He was just coming off of a two-game suspension for drinking at a party a year ago, and was looking forward to finally getting to play football. I did remember that night when he came home, because I was still up (so it wasn't terribly late) and we talked when he came in the house. He seemed perfectly sober to me, and I didn't even question if he'd been drinking that night – it was obvious to me he hadn't.

Anyway, the school questioned everyone who had been at

the party, including Michael and his best friend. They all said the same thing. Those who were drinking denied it (most of them did at least – two of them confessed), and they all said who else had been there. They all said that Michael and his best friend had not been drinking.

Well, the school decided to punish those boys for 'being at a party where there was alcohol.' But they didn't give any punishment (that I know of) to all of the other kids who were actually drinking and hadn't confessed, because they said they couldn't prove that they actually were – even though the other kids all told me they had said those kids were drinking, a lot. I asked why they didn't punish them the same as Michael, for just being there. They said they were taking care of it, and other kids' punishment was not my business. They were right. My only business was with my son.

Anyway, after it was over, Michael and his friend had to sit on the sidelines for being at a party where there was alcohol, and watch their friends play, a lot of whom had been there too, drunk.

I went to the school board to voice my displeasure with how the situation was handled.

It was very emotional for me, because I knew Michael drank. But I had to stick up for him this time since he told me he hadn't been drinking. Michael was not a liar. If he would have been drinking, he would have admitted it to me, and he would have gotten punished from me. Happened before, and he knew it. He also had to know that if he had been wrongly accused, that I would stop at nothing to defend his honor. That's what I was doing then.

I was told that they were making an example out of Michael, hoping to deter other kids from even being at a party where there was alcohol. They said that the right thing would have been for Michael to leave right away, and not stay for any amount of time.

I was also told that I should be grateful, because by Michael getting punished, and the others not, it might end up saving his life someday.

Is this irony at its best or what? Every single one of the other kids is alive today. And Michael is dead.

Well, I've decided to make an example of Michael myself. I will defend his "underage stupidity" as long as it takes to get things to change with regard to those "adults" who buy alcohol for minors. Nothing may get done with the individual who specifically bought the alcohol that Michael drank that took his life, but I don't think I can feel good about myself, or the future safety of Matt and all of the boys' friends that I dearly love and care about, if I just sit back and do nothing.

With prayerful guidance from God, I will do what is right – as Michael's "example."

Friday, July 28, 2006
The heat is becoming bad. We've had 100 degree + days for many days now. And there doesn't seem to be much relief in sight.

I know this sounds eccentric, but I can find a relation to virtually every single thing that happens in my day, right down to the weather, to something about Michael.

Michael loved the heat. I don't ever remember him complaining about hot weather. He loved having his room hot in the winter. I used to go in his room to wake him up in the morning and he would have the thermometer turned up to over 80 degrees. I'd turn it down right before we left for the day, and he'd always grumble. He wanted it hot during the day so it would be hot that night when he went to bed. I felt sometimes like I was going to suffocate when I was in there. When he was in the hospital I always made sure his blanket covered him up, right down to his toes. I knew he liked to be warm. I don't think he would have minded the hot weather we're having now.

Roger wants us to plant a tree by his grave so that someday it will give him shade. I don't think that's very realistic because there is no water at the cemetery, and it's too dry, even if we haul water there everyday. But maybe someday.

I guess when I'm out there, it is very hot, and sunny, but I just don't think Michael would have minded it. It's the cold and snow I worry about this winter. Funny, isn't it – the things we spend time worrying about. I know – Michael's body can't feel heat or cold.

I know – he's gone. I know – it's just his body in that coffin in the ground. Yet I know – that grave is where the physical him is left. I can't touch him, but I know he's there. His body is there.

That's why I was so determined to give him the casket we did. The metal ones were less expensive, but I couldn't let him be buried in cold metal. He had to have wood – that was him – it was warm. I had to make sure the cloth inside was soft, and didn't sound crunchy. Yes, some of the material in the caskets sounded crunchy and harsh. It had to feel soft, and warm.

I've tried to protect his body since the second he was born. I've spent 18 years trying to make him comfortable. It's a hard habit to break.

Monday, July 31, 2006

I admit it. I have had the worst four days, I think, since Michael died. I can't seem to get anything accomplished. I just want to cry. Sometimes I don't even want to, and I do. I feel guilty if I've done something, and I feel guilty if I haven't done something. There is no balance at all with how I feel lately. It's up and down, and sometimes just plain out of control.

I really thought that by now I should be feeling better, and that it would be getting easier. It isn't, usually. Maybe it's a combination of being busy, the drought, the heat – it's all starting to just trap me.

I read about a family that lost a child, and three weeks later they took a vacation, camping. I remember thinking at the time 'how could they do that. How could they act like everything was normal, and go camping?' Now I understand, I think. I feel like I just want to get away. Part of me wants to take Roger and Matt, and part of me doesn't. I think I'd like to just go someplace where it's nice and quiet, and there's no one around wanting to know how I'm doing.

I even feel guilty about telling people how I'm doing. Yesterday I might have told someone "pretty good" and today they see me and I'm a mess. I hope everyone understands that I'm not being dishonest, things just change with me at a drop of a hat!

Believe me, I don't like it!

I didn't go to the cemetery today. I probably should have, but I just couldn't. It's hard going there, but I usually don't mind because sometimes I just have to be close. Today, I couldn't. But at least I knew that. Maybe that's a good sign?

My mind knows where Michael is. My mind knows that he's better now than he's ever been. My mind knows that he is at peace. My heart just can't get any of that figured out yet. It's not real pleasant when your mind and your heart are at such odds.

God willing, the sun will rise tomorrow. God willing, tomorrow will be an easier day to get through. If not, I guess, there's always the next day.

Chapter 4

Tuesday, August 1, 2006

We had .15" on rain last night. We were ready to build an ark! It's the first we've had in close to six weeks. Plus, the temperature topped today at around 85 degrees. It's been a very pleasant day.

Matt and I sat outside during the rain last night. There can't be anything in the world more calming than a very gentle rain at night. It was so quiet. Then – a bat flew through the porch area, so Matt, just like a little kid would do, got a fish net out of the garage and waited to catch that bat! Thankfully it didn't happen. I asked him what he was going to do with the bat if he actually caught it, and he said he'd figure that out if he did. It was fun. It was normal – just, without Michael there.

Roger came outside a little later, and as I sat there and watched the two of them, I thought – this is it. This is all I have left at home. Now, I know that sounds bad, and ungrateful. Maybe it's a strange kind of empty-nest feeling. When Amber left home, it was for a good thing, to go to college. I was expecting Michael to leave home, too, to go to college. I was looking forward to it! It was going to be great – only having to cook for the three of us, only having to clean for the three of us. Now, I'm there, but for all the wrong reasons. He's gone, but not for a good thing; at least not a good earthly thing. And Matt – now he's so close to leaving home too. I'm just not ready for anymore "gones".

You dream as your kids get older of them leaving home, then coming home to visit, then bringing little ones back with them. That's what Amber did. It's what I expected Michael to do someday. It's what I want Matt to do, someday. But Michael won't be coming back to visit, let alone bring anyone else with him. Ever. Ever is a very long time.

I think that's what is so depressing. We live in such a "hurry up" society, and for as much as I know that I will one day see Michael again, I want it to "hurry up." I also know that in my "want" for life to "hurry up" I could very well miss out on the life that is "now." I'm trying. I'm really trying.

Today was a good and sunny day, because of all the clouds! God's blessings to everyone.

Wednesday, August 2, 2006

I've realized today, again, just how much I have to have God in my life right now.

I keep thinking about the *Footprints* story. It was one of my grandpa's favorites. Grandpa never seemed to show his faith and religion outwardly, at least not in front of me. But he always said he loved this story and had a print of it framed in his house. I have one too, and it always makes me think of him. This simple show of faith on his part really made an impact on me when I was younger, and it still does now. Now I read it with such understanding.

I can honestly say that since Michael's accident, I have not been angry with him, or with God. Michael, like grandpa, didn't show his faith outwardly all the time. But I remember while taking his senior pictures, that he was very concerned about having the cross on his bull bell showing. He went to a Cowboys for Christ camp a couple of times, and kept up with their newsletters and internet information. His faith was simple, yet I know it was there. Everyone always says they think their loved one is now in Heaven after they've died, or that they hope that's where they're at – but I don't think that kind of hope is enough. You have to know! That is so very much the most important thing! And when you know, it helps. As hard as it has been to lose Michael, I can't imagine wondering if he was really in Heaven. And I can't imagine not knowing that God is with me, helping me get through this.

I'm confident too, that God was carrying Michael to Heaven on May 17, 2006.

God's blessings to us all.

Thursday, August 3, 2006

The Navy wants Michael. But then, so do a lot of people and companies. The Marines want him. Loaning institutions are still lined up to offer him low interest student loans to pay for college. Then there are the credit card companies – he could have a line of credit up to $10,000 today – it's been pre-approved! All he has to do is sign it and send it back!

Michael did have some clothing store credit card. When he died he owed around $95. I paid it and asked them to cancel it because he had died. They want a copy of the death certificate as proof. For crying out loud, the bill is paid. I just want them to stop sending zero balance statements and increasing his line of credit!

Then today, another bank called and asked for Michael. I paused, and told them he had died. The guy immediately asked for the name and phone number of the funeral home, for verification. I told them I was his mother, and wanted to know what business they had with Michael. They told me it was with regard to a credit card bill that he hasn't paid in three months (gee, I wonder why). I asked the specifics of the name of the card, and they told me they could only talk to Michael. Again, I said he had died. Again, they wanted the name and phone number of the funeral home, for verification. They said if I didn't give it to them, they would continue to call for five more months. Yeah, they won't believe me, his mother, that he's dead, but will believe the funeral home. I wanted to scream – you idiots! Come live inside my head and heart for a minute – you'll believe he's gone! The guy said that once they had verification that he was dead, they would make a claim against his estate.

I almost choked laughing. Estate? Michael? Eighteen years old? The local bank's overdraft person of the year? I'll never pay Michael's bill to that place – if they are even legitimate.

How often do these things happen to kids? I'll bet a lot. Here's Michael, a young 18 year old high school kid, with no job, no assets (except that car - the boat - worth a whopping $200 after the two new $60 tires were put on it), and a credit card company tells him he has impeccable credit and gives him a card with a large limit on it. Then he dies. Where do they think their money is going to come from? When Michael was overdrawn at the bank, who transferred money to cover the charges? Mom. But who will this company not take the word of when she tells them Michael is dead? Mom.

Guess they're going to be calling me for the next five months, because this mom has no intentions of paying a bill to a company that exploited her minor child in the first place, and won't even take her word that he is dead!

I almost enjoy having these places act like jerks. It gives me a place to channel my anger. Yes, I feel angry. Even though I honestly have never felt anger with Michael or with God, I've wanted to be angry at "something."

Well, bring it on, credit card companies. I think you're being very therapeutic for me!

God bless everyone!

Friday, August 4, 2006

I wondered tonight if I make people uncomfortable when I talk about Michael. I think I've talked about him and told stories about him quite a bit this week. Sometimes I cry when I talk about him, but mostly I've been just remembering fun times. When other people used to do that, when they had someone very close to them die, I would never know what to say. I admit that it used to make me feel strange – and often I just wouldn't say anything back. Now, I'm on the other side. So, I apologize if it makes others feel strange. But sometimes I just have to talk about him. I have to remember him. And I have to learn to do it without crying.

I've read some very inspiring stories from other people who have lost a child. I would begin reading and think – oh, those poor people, their child is dead. Then I read further, and they write about their feelings and I think – wow, that's exactly how I feel!

The only thing I've read lately that I don't completely feel comfortable with is people who use mediums to communicate with their dead children. In one article, the lady even talked very matter-of-factly about how her dead son still talked to her, and "is just as talkative as ever." I couldn't do that. I think someone like that might be in denial yet. Religiously, it's something I was brought up to stay away from. And I will. Instead, I'll trust and have faith in God that Michael is just fine. I want to talk to him, and sometimes I do, but I certainly don't expect him to talk back

110

to me – himself or through anyone else.

I want him here, but he isn't. As reality sets in more each day, I think I seek more memories. And I sometimes have a desire to share them.

Thank you for listening – in person, or here in the journal.

God's blessings to us all.

Saturday, August 5, 2006

I went to a family reunion today. I don't especially like being around a lot of people lately, especially family. Everyone tries to be thoughtful and caring, but sometimes I feel light-headed and almost like I can't breath. So I tried to be late. It didn't work. I had the wrong time down to be there, and I was actually early.

I cried almost all the way there. I think part of that is because I took my Jeep. I haven't driven it much lately because the car gets better gas mileage, and Matt's been driving the Jeep. I kept looking over at the passenger side. I remember driving to town every day this past year with the boys.

Michael hated getting up in the morning. He was like me – a night owl. Anyway, it was such an effort to get him going in the morning, and he really never cared if he was late for school or not! Matt, on the other hand, couldn't stand it if he was late! Michael always took a shower in the morning, and since we always seemed to be running late, he never dried his hair before we would leave. He'd get into the front seat of the Jeep, wearing his cap (which he always had on), take it off and shake his head like a dog. I used to even tell him he looked like a dog shaking to dry off. Then he'd put his cap back on, over his face, and settle into the seat to sleep on the way to town. When I'd pull up in front of the school, he'd do it again – take off the cap, shake his head for the final drying, put his cap back on, and go inside.

During the drive today I just kept looking at that empty seat, but it was like I could see him sitting there, or actually, laying back in the seat sleeping!

It just made me feel very sad.

The reunion ended up being very nice, and I was glad I wasn't late. I had a chance to visit with some second cousins that I haven't seen in a long time.

It was easier on the way home, but still kind of sad and tearful.

Matt went with some other kids to a movie tonight. I feel very strange about that. It's the first Saturday night he's gone out since Michael's accident, and he never went out much at all before then either. I know I can't keep him locked up, but I don't think I'll be able to sleep until he's home in bed. I'm trying very hard not to suffocate him right now. It's good that he's out with some other kids. I just can't quit praying for their safety tonight.

Today's message says – Sit quietly in My presence. Take time to rest by the wayside, for I am not in a hurry. When you rush, you forget who you are and whose you are.

Once again, good words.

Sunday, August 6, 2006

Matt and I went to Rapid City today. We must be gluttons for punishment. The traffic was horrendous–motorcycles everywhere.

I'm glad we spent the day together. I've wondered lately if I neglect him now by always thinking about Michael. I've always loved my kids equally, but now that Michael's gone, he's the one I think about constantly. Why is that? I can't do anything for him now. So why is so much of my conscious consumed with him? I don't think it means I actually loved him more than Matt or Amber, but I don't know what it means. Maybe it's normal. That's a scary thought too. I don't want to ever forget Michael. But I also don't want to think about him so constantly. It's very tiring. But I can't help it. It just happens.

When we used to watch Michael at rodeos, I never thought about Matt much. And when we were watching Matt at basketball games, I never thought much about Michael. I guess I was never very worried about any of the kids. But now, everything brings up a memory or thought of Michael. Is that good? I don't know.

God bless everyone tonight.

Monday, August 7, 2006

A little over a year after Roger and I were married, we found out Michael was on the way, and we were thrilled. Roger wanted a son so badly. I actually thought a little boy would be kind of boring. Little girls were fun. You could dress them up so cute, and they liked cute little toys. Mid-way through my pregnancy, I had an ultrasound. The doctor anticipated the gender of the baby and wrote it down on paper and sealed it in an envelope. He said that way we wouldn't have to know unless we chose to. I took the envelope home and showed it to Roger. He immediately opened it. He really wanted to know! He wasn't disappointed at all – he was getting a son.

Roger had decided almost from day one that if the baby was a boy he wanted to name him after his grandfather – Mike Glynn – who was the first Glynn to live on our ranch. Roger loved his grandfather deeply, and wanted his son to be able to carry on the "Mike Glynn" name on the ranch someday.

So, for the next four months we waited anxiously for Michael to be born - for him to take his first breath of air, for his first day at home with us, for his first smile, for his first everything. It happened on August 7, 1987 at 9:55 p.m.

As soon as he was born I realized how wrong I had been about little boys. He was a thrill! He was adorable. He was fun. He was funny. He was the apple of his daddy's eye. He was (along with Amber, so far) the love of my life.

Eighteen years, 9 months and ten days later, I waited patiently in a hospital room for Michael to die - to take his last breath of air, for his first day at home with God in Heaven.

I can still feel his birth. And I can feel his death. A mother shouldn't be able to feel both!

It's not supposed to be like this!

He was supposed to sit by me with his kids and maybe even grandkids and watch me die, an old woman who had lived a beautiful life. He was supposed to plan my funeral, and say it was a blessing because I had become so old that my body was worn out, and I was ready to spend eternity in Heaven.

Nothing is the way it should be, especially today.

Tonight Roger, Matt and I went to the cemetery. We took 19 helium balloons, and one by one we sent them flying to the clouds. We sent 19 kisses to Michael, one for each year old he would have been today. We must have been at the cemetery for over two hours, because a bunch of Michael's friends showed up. We all cried, we hugged, and we remembered Michael. It was a beautiful ending to a very sad and hard day. How can we be so blessed to have such wonderful people in our lives, as they were in Michael's lives?

God is truly good. All the time.

Tuesday, August 8, 2006

I don't know the exact reason, but I feel good tonight. The fact that we just had .81" of rain probably helped! Matt is spending the night at a friend's house because they have to leave really early tomorrow morning to help someone work cattle. So, I had to watch the storm come in by myself. Actually, I spent more time watching it leave. Watching it roll in was kind of scary – it was extremely windy and the lightning was terrible. After the rain I went outside and just thanked! I felt so close to Michael. As usual, I was fixated on the clouds, and believing Michael was watching us from them.

I wondered – when we get to Heaven, aren't we supposed to be made aware of "all the answers"? Since God made us in His image, when we get to Heaven, will we be God-like? I guess I'm not really sure, and I hope I'm not having sacrilegious thoughts. But I wondered, while watching those Heavenly clouds, and smelling that wonderfully fragrant moisture, maybe being closer to God makes me closer to Michael. I'm certainly not saying that I think Michael has become God, but they are together now, more so than ever. I've known that for weeks now, but for some reason tonight it felt like it just finally really hit me. It felt good.

A friend e-mailed today and talked about feelings of guilt and doubt, and where they originate. Yes, they are spawned from evil. I've told that to countless people, yet it's very reassuring to hear it said to me. And yes, the closer you get to God, the less happy evil is and the harder evil works to move you away from God. It's

114

hard, without a doubt.

But if I've learned anything the past two days, it's that God has given me extraordinary friends who have been there, are there now, and I know will continue to be there for me. How could I ever turn my back on the One that has so graciously blessed me this way?

I have to keep focused, and remember that God did not cause Michael to die. There were evil forces at work that caused the accident to happen. I believe that God only allowed Michael to die because he loved him so much he gave him free will to make choices. I also believe that God must have cried when Michael died, but also instantly forgave him for making the wrong choice of drinking and driving that led to his death. Then, I believe when the whole situation was out of Michael's hands – that's when God did start causing some very good things to happen because of his death.

I believe that Michael's purpose in life was to make lots of friends and have many, many people love him. God knew this would happen, and he knew he would then be using all of us to carry on with His message of salvation.

Maybe my most important purpose in life was to give birth to this wonderful person, who would through his death, become a messenger of God.

I pray for everyone to feel as blessed as I do tonight.

Wednesday, August 9, 2006

When I was coming home from work tonight, Matt and two of his friends were parked on the side of the road; one of the friend's pickup was stalled. The boys were trying to figure out just what to do. They decided to take Matt's pickup back to town to get some tools to try and get the other pickup fixed. When I left and looked in the rear-view mirror at them, it just made me smile. They have been the "little boys" for so long, and now they're learning how to become men. For so many years, I have watched Matt and Michael do these same things together, and now I'm watching Matt grow up with his friends, kind of taking Michael's place. Yeah, those boys were broke down on the side of the road, but they weren't worried. They had a plan, and they were having fun. It just made me smile!

It also reminded me of something that happened after the State B basketball tournament this year. We came home from Aberdeen in a blizzard, and were stranded in Chamberlain for an additional night. I was able to get a room, but in my effort to save money, I crowded myself and five teenaged boys into just one room. I told Roger later that I wouldn't do that again. Next year if it happens, I'll spring for two or even three rooms! Those boys were going stir crazy in that hotel all day and evening. But, back to the story.

All afternoon people kept coming into the hotel as they were stopped on the Interstate. I watched them drive in and park in the parking lot, slipping and sliding on the snow and ice, and praying they wouldn't hit my vehicle. There was one couple that gave us pure entertainment. They had a U-Haul truck (a small one) and were pulling a trailer with a small car on it.

They couldn't get it parked. The lady was outside trying to direct the man into a spot, and it just wouldn't work. So he got out and had her drive. She wasn't any better. She kept backing up, going forward, turning the steering wheel the wrong direction, and jack-knifing the truck and trailer.

Finally, after close to an hour of watching this fiasco, Michael couldn't take it either. On crutches (he was recuperating from a broken ankle), he hobbled out there in the snow and ice and tried to tell them how to turn their steering wheel to make it work. The man treated Michael (I thought) like he was just a stupid kid. But that "stupid kid" knew what he was talking about. They were just uppity-acting city folks (with out-of-state-plates) who don't know how our country kids are raised! I heard (I had the window open and was listening to and watching the whole ordeal) Michael then tell them to just unhook the trailer and push it where they wanted it to go. The guy did try that, but couldn't get the hitch to un-hitch.

About that time, the rest of the boys who were staying with me had all gone down to see the commotion. Michael told the lady where to drive towards, and the other boys all pushed and steered the trailer, with the car on it and still hitched to the truck. It finally got parked, in less than five minutes!

The boys came back up to the room and acted like what they had done was all in a day's work. For them, it was. Those are good kids!

Another fairly good day, another really good memory.

Blessings to all!

Friday, August 11, 2006

I missed writing in the journal last night! A storm came through and knocked our electricity out for a few hours.

I've had such a good couple of days. I've decided that I'm tired of having bad weekends at home. I'm trying very hard to be positive and optimistic so that I can actually accomplish something and enjoy this weekend.

This morning before I left for work I went into Michael's room, just to sit on the bed and breathe him in. I realized that it's usually how I start my Saturday mornings, and when I eventually pull myself out of the room, I've already cried at least once. This morning I only stayed in there for a few minutes, before I started getting teary-eyed. I'm going to try doing that from now on – just staying in there a short time. Maybe if I do that a few times, it'll be easier to stay longer. It's a plan, at least.

Monday we're going to Pierre to meet with the Highway Patrol regarding their new *Parents Matter* campaign to educate kids about the dangers of drinking and driving. I'm hopeful that the media will pick up on the campaign also, and help to get the message out. We're also meeting with a radio station in Pierre. I'm looking forward to it. It will feel good to feel like I'm doing something worthwhile. I just really don't want Michael to have died, without somebody else learning from his mistakes.

Okay, here comes the weekend. And I'm ready.

God bless everyone tonight, and give a special thanks for the rain that has found its way to our area!

Saturday, August 12, 2006

I'm trying. I'm really trying. Today didn't go like I wanted it to. But then, how often do we really get our own way? I was dusting in the living room this morning, and there is Michael – pictures everywhere. It can be so hard to look at his pictures. I mean, he's right there, looking back at me. I feel like I should be able to reach out and touch him. It was only a few weeks ago that a lot of those pictures were taken.

I keep thinking when I look at the pictures – he had so much going for him; he was good-looking, he was smart (when he wanted to be), he was charismatic (boy, was he ever!), he was talented, he was confident, he had parents who would give him anything he needed, he had friends and family who loved and adored him. Yet, what he thought he needed, to have a good time, was alcohol. My God, the control it has over our youth is staggering!!! And it killed him. He is dead. His dreams are gone, and our dreams for him are dead.

Do you have any idea how mad that makes me? I mean, I spent years and years coddling that child, worrying about him and his needs, protecting him - all those things wrapped up in "loving him." And just like that, alcohol comes into his life and just rips him away from me – forever. How can I ever forgive alcohol for doing that? Someone or something has to take the blame for this. Someone or something has to be held responsible.

I was in his room for quite a while tonight. Again, it still looks like his room, smells like it; makes it hard to understand that he's gone. I've been re-reading the hospital reports from the Rosebud Hospital. I want them to make sense. I want to understand every single thing that was happening with him while he was there. It's hard to read and understand. Why do I want to do this? I don't know. It's not like it will change anything. I just want to know.

I am not going overboard in my quest to stop this from ever happening again. When our children do something wrong, like color on a wall, do we just say once "don't do that" and let them color on it the next time?

When we, as messengers of God, tell someone about salvation, do we just say it once and forget about it? Or do we talk about it as often as we can, as often as it takes to make someone believe? Shouldn't we do the same with alcohol? Can we just say "don't do it" and feel like we've done all we can? Or do we keep saying it over and over again until someone believes?

It's hard. I personally hate having to repeat myself. I want people to hear me the first time, don't argue, and just do as I say. But that doesn't happen very often. So why should we expect it to happen that way with our kids? They need repetition. They need continuity.

Okay, the weekend is only half over. And it hasn't been that bad. I've had worse lately. I'm looking forward to tomorrow. I need to look forward to each day's rising sun!

God bless everyone. Remember – John 3:16.

Sunday, August 13, 2006

Last night Matt and I watched a movie, where in the end a young boy was killed in a gang-related drive-by shooting. It was sad, so sad. They showed a lot of the funeral in the show. I cried, but not like usual during sad movies. I cried for Michael. I ended up sleeping in his room for about half of the night then. But I slept with one of the windows partially opened.

I realized this weekend that I'm drawn to his room. I think it's because I have kept the door closed all this time, trying to keep his scent in the room - trying to keep him there. I think that's why, when I go by the door, I have such an overwhelming desire to go in, then stay too long, then feel bad.

So, when I left the room last night, I left the door open and the window up. The door and window have been open all day today too. And, amazingly, I'm okay with that. In fact, it's been good.

I know it's going to make Michael's scent leave more quickly. But is it really "Michael's" scent? I mean, it's basically the scent of leather and branding. It's just that those smells resonate with him so easily. Maybe if the door is open, and it becomes a room, rather than just Michael's room, I'll do better when I'm in there. I also think its time to finish taking his things off the walls in there.

119

It's my plan for next weekend, maybe, or the next. I don't know when. I guess it just feels better to actually understand that I need to do it.

Tuesday, August 15, 2006

It's been exactly three months. Three months since Michael's accident. Three months ago we were with him in the hospital, knowing that he was hurt bad, but truly believing he would be okay. I just knew that nothing as devastating as dying would happen to Michael. I barely even gave it a thought. I was actually thinking about how I was going to schedule being in Sioux Falls for days, or even weeks with him as he got better and underwent various therapies. What proof this is that we are not in control!

Yesterday I spent most of the day in Pierre. A neighbor had suggested possibly getting in touch with the media to do some public service announcements reminding kids to not drink and drive. We met with the radio station, then with the Highway Patrol and Department of Public Safety. It was a good day, but kind of hard, and very tiring. My head was throbbing by the time I headed back home.

It was decided that myself and Matt (he doesn't know it yet – I'm going to use the element of surprise!) are going to do some radio spots, talking about what this had done to us, from a very personal perspective – the mother and the brother. They want to get these started so they can be aired before and during the state 4-h rodeo finals. They also suggested putting banners up, similar to the sponsors banners, as reminders to the kids of what can happen if they drink and drive.

The Department of Public Safety and the Highway Patrol are beginning a *Parents Matter* campaign. They explained some of the education and media plans they have, as well as a new web-site. The web-site is very good in my opinion. It's very informative and extremely easy to navigate and read. Go to www.state. sd.us/dps/ and click on Parents Matter.

They asked my permission to use Michael's photo and the picture of his car in some of their ads and announcements. Of course,

I said yes. I think I'll be doing some other things with this campaign in the future, just not sure what, when and where yet. I guess you could say we spent the afternoon brainstorming ideas.

Today I was contacted by a radio station in Sioux Falls, and will be doing an interview with them later this week. They're going to do about the same thing as the station in Pierre will be doing. They think it will help to have kids hear from the actual mother of a kid that a lot of kids in this state knew, or at least know someone who knew him . . .

I just feel like I have to do something. I still think if I'd have told Michael more often, or more sternly, that he simply shouldn't drink alcohol, because it's illegal and harmful to minors, maybe I could have gotten through to him and he would be here today. But, since I didn't, I feel like I need to for Matt and all of the other kids out there who are still wandering, and wondering, about the choices they should make.

I want them to remember Michael. I want them to learn from his mistakes. His death has to count for at least that. He can't die for nothing. I just won't let it! Other young lives have got to be saved!

I pray that God will lead me to do His will, in all of my endeavors.

Wednesday, August 16, 2006

Today was strange. It was one of those days that emotions were bouncing off the wall. I thought a lot today about what I might say during the radio interview tomorrow morning. Actually, I came up with something that sounded great at about 3:00 a.m. this morning when I couldn't sleep. Instead of getting up and writing it down, I went into Michael's room to sleep. I fell asleep and slept like a baby – all of three hours!

I want so badly to simply say "don't drink" rather than "if you drink, don't drive." I don't want kids to drink, period! I mean, what really is the point of saying "if you drink, just don't drive." That's exactly what we said to Michael the night of May 14, 2006 – the last thing we ever said to him that he acknowledged. He said, "ok." But he did drink. And he drove. And he died. So what good did it do to say that to him? We have asked ourselves a million times – why didn't he just stay in town like we told him to? Why did he try to drive home when we told him not to? When he was in the hospital I couldn't wait for him to wake up to answer that question. He never did. He was never able to tell us himself.

But now, I think I might understand why he chose to try coming home that morning.

His mind was impaired. He couldn't think clearly. He wasn't able to reason. Why? Isn't it obvious? These are all the things that are preached to all of us, constantly, as the effects of drinking alcohol! How could we have expected him to even remember what we had told him the night before? It doesn't work that way when you're drunk. And I would challenge anyone who has ever been drunk to deny it.

Do we really think that when we tell our kids, "if you drink, just don't drive" that they'll remember that when they're drunk? Being drunk loosens you up. It makes you feel relaxed and comfortable. It makes kids feel like they're invincible.

Do you know how many times my kids have said to me, "but mom, you just don't understand how it is in the real world." Dozens – hundreds of times – when they were stone-sober! They just don't think us old-fogies (anyone over the golden age of 30) are very smart. So why would we expect them to think we're smart and have intelligent advice to offer, when they're drunk and think they're on top of the world?

I guess I shouldn't always be using the word "drunk" either. Kids don't have to be "drunk" to be "under the influence." Any amount of alcohol in their blood is illegal! There is no legally allowable amount for minors like there is for adults.

I hear quite often, " yeah, but peer pressure is strong, and they're going to drink anyway, we all know it, they just need to make a good choice and not drive if they do." Well, I used to be one that said that. And look at me now. My family is broken. I have a hole in my heart that will never, ever heal. I will live with this guilt, fear, sadness and pain every day for the rest of my life.

You may see me outwardly laughing or smiling, but deep inside my heart I constantly cry.

I'm sorry, but I can not be asked to say "If you drink, don't drive." I can only say "don't drink, period" and if no one wants to listen, I'm very sorry. From what has happened to my family, it doesn't do any good to say "if." Please, don't be the next family that has to repeat my life from May 15, 2006 on. It is not fun.

By the way – I prayed often today, asking God's guidance in what I would write in today's journal. I feel comfortable with what I said, and I will continue to ask God to keep me strong, and not let the world influence me into changing my thoughts – those which have been directed from Him.

With God ALL things are possible!!

Thursday, August 17, 2006
Today is going to go down as one of those really, really bad days.

I think I got myself all worked up this morning, being nervous about that damned radio interview. Part of me says I wish I'd never agreed to do it. Another part says "just suck it up, Joyce, and start dealing with things." I have these two parts of me that spend a lot of time arguing with each other. The interview went as I thought it would; I was asked questions, I answered, I choked up, I sniffled, my throat quivered, and the second I hung up the phone I burst into tears. I'm not sure now I could even recall all I said.

Then, I felt the brunt of a very upset customer. It left a bad feeling in the pit of my stomach that lasted the rest of the morning.

I kept watching the clock, like I tend to do on these significant days. Michael officially died three months ago today, at 2:36 p.m. Around 2:00 I felt like I'd been totally unproductive (as usual these past few days). I left and went to visit a friend. When I got back in the car, it was after 2:36. I had missed it. I felt like I couldn't breathe. My whole body shook and I cried uncontrollably – all the way to the cemetery. I pulled a few weeds and straightened up the flower arrangements that had fallen over and brushed the dirt off of them. Maybe I missed the time today because in my heart

I know he died earlier than the "declared" time. I know when he was really gone, and it was 12:35.

Then it was back to the office. A friend came in shortly after that and told me she had come across an old newspaper that had been tucked away in her house. She had no idea why she saved it. She said she started looking through it for an article she may have wanted to clip, and the only thing she found that was significant to her was the Student of the Week article. That week it was Michael. The year was 2000; he was in sixth grade. She said she believes there was a reason God had her save that paper six years ago. She said He knew then what was going to happen to Michael, and that it would make me smile on this dreary day for her to find that simple little article and give it to me. She was right. It made me smile! Really, it made me laugh. Listen to a portion of what his principle wrote at the end – "Michael is a very quiet serious boy." Michael? Quiet? Serious? About school? Boy, did he change by the time he was through with high school! Seriously though, it went on to say "he is a good student, good athlete, and more important, a very outstanding well-mannered young man. He will go far in this world of ours as he knows the meaning of hard work and being responsible."

Well, Michael didn't have time in our world to go very far. But I believe he's soaring in Heaven.

The best thing about a day like today? Tomorrow has to be better. That's what I'm going to look forward to.

God is good, all the time – All the time, God is good.

Friday, August 18, 2006

Yep, I was right. Today was a better day than yesterday, for me anyway.

It started out a little rocky though. I was sent an e-mail that I just had to share it with Roger this morning. It made both of us tear up, and Roger doesn't do that often. Tonight I've re-read it a few times, and I just smile. That's the way my life is now, though. One day I can laugh at the very same thing I cried at the day before. I never know when, and what, something will trigger a feeling, or it's opposite.

This weekend is Frontier Days, and that alone has me a little on edge. The theme of the parade tomorrow is "Year of the Cowboy." Well, obviously, my favorite cowboy won't be here.

Here is a brief synopsis of what was e-mailed to me: She was behind the chutes waiting to watch Michael ride. She said she was getting nervous, and about 15 minutes before the bull riding, Michael was lying along the back fence sleeping. She said she went over to him, kicked him and told him he only had about15 minutes left. He looked up at her and said, "good, I've still got ten minutes of good sleeping time left." He ended up riding and winning first place!

That was SO Michael. He was so layed back and confident in himself.

I remember back when he was in fifth grade. He used to wear a western shirt and boots to school every day! One of his teachers told me that he was proud of Michael, because some of the other kids started making fun of him for dressing like that, and he never budged. He was who he was, and he was happy with that. His teacher told me that because Michael didn't even flinch when they teased him, it wasn't long before they quit. Soon, he was admired because he was "always a cowboy." Of course, he did get to the point that he wore tennis shoes and t-shirts to school most of the time, but it was when he wanted to, and not when others made him feel like he should.

I was, and still am, proud of his confidence and leadership. But I sometimes think that's also what made him think he was invincible – even enough so that he thought he could drink and drive and nothing would hurt him. I think it's a very fine line, and one day Michael crossed over – thanks to a bunch of alcohol-induced dead brain cells.

It's going to be a sad day for our family to celebrate the "Year of the Cowboy" tomorrow.

May God's abundant blessings be seen and felt by everyone.

Saturday, August 19, 2006

Frontier Days is half over. Just one more rodeo performance tomorrow, then the 4-h finals next weekend and White River's Little Britches rodeo a couple of weeks after that. Then, I think we're pretty well finished with rodeos for the season. I'm ready. I get these horrible headaches during rodeos now. Some people have said it's a kind of "grief expression" because it was such a huge part of Michael's life.

The American Legion and Rodeo Committee purchased the most beautiful buckle I have ever seen, in memory of Michael, to present to the winner of the bull riding this weekend. Only three of ten riders rode today. They rode well, but I thought the judges were judging a little low. They are the same judges as last year, and the high point today was 74. Last year Michael won with a 77. I'm kind of secretly hoping that someone who rides tomorrow will win, so they'll be there to get that buckle in person. I'd like to see them. I hope it's someone who knew Michael. That would make it even more meaningful.

I think I'm too tired tonight to write much. It's been a hard day emotionally.

You know, it just occurred to me that I didn't go to the cemetery today. I was going to make sure and do that, and I forgot. I wonder what it means when I start forgetting that?

Matt went to the mud races tonight, but I wouldn't let him stay in for the dance. I'm just not ready to let him go someplace like that where there will be a lot of older kids around there, probably drinking. I'm fearful of accidents and such tonight, and I just wanted him home where I think he's safe. He didn't even argue when he called to ask and I said no. He just came home. Now that everyone's here and safe, I think I can sleep. Tomorrow will be another long day.

God's blessings to all.

Sunday, August 20, 2006

I have no energy today. It's just after noon and I let Roger and Matt go in to the rodeo themselves. I told them I'd come in later, in time for the bull riding and slack. I have a horrible headache and my legs feel like jelly. I just can't hardly take this weekend.

Last night when we were coming home we saw a couple of deer – does, each with two little ones. They were adorable! I commented on how cute they were and Roger just talked about how we're getting too many of them again, and all the fence he has to fix because of them. He's right. But then he said they might be what caused Michael's accident. Someone did say there were deer in a pasture near the spot Michael ran off the road that morning, and maybe he simply swerved to avoid them on the highway. Last night Roger thought maybe that's what really happened. I reminded him of how much alcohol was in Michael's blood, and he just said that he knew Michael was drinking a lot less this year than he did last year, and that he'd come home before after drinking and he knew how to handle himself. I guess I don't care how much less Michael was drinking this year, he was still drinking that night. And he was drinking a lot!

Do you have any idea how I'd like to think that Michael's accident was totally not his fault? That it was the fault of the car? That it was the fault of deer? That it was the fault of the law enforcement for not picking him up before he got out of town? That it was the fault of the other kids for letting him drive? That it was the fault of society?

Ultimately, it was him, and us. We let him behave like that. And he chose to drink that much alcohol – he chose to drink, period. And we chose to allow it. At least, that's my opinion.

I don't know. Roger seems, outwardly at least, to be handling things much better than me. I feel like a mess most of the time. Maybe his believing in the "deer theory" is what gets him through this nightmare. Maybe I should concoct a "deer theory" of my own. Maybe I have, in the alcohol, and I'm the one who is misled. I don't know. I just don't know. I don't feel like I know anything anymore.

Well, it's evening now, and we just got back from the rodeo. As soon as the slack started, it started pouring rain. It was wonderful. I don't know if it was the rain, or just time, but I feel better tonight than I did this afternoon.

God, please stay with me now, and give me strength.

Wednesday, August 23, 2006

I think I've had about 12 hours sleep in the past three nights. Then, I was sick to my stomach Tuesday morning, which is not a good day to feel lousy at my job. Last night I hoped to get to bed early, and I came home to a horrendous lightning and wind storm. Fortunately, there weren't any fires in the area, but Roger and Matt were out very late watching, and I couldn't sleep anyway until they came home. I think I'm running on fumes. On the up-side – when you're this busy and tired you don't have the time or energy to feel sorry for yourself!

But I have to say, I'm getting tired of rodeos this summer. They've been good, and I'm glad we've been going to quite a few, but I'm getting exhausted by them. It is just so hard to not be there to watch Michael. I still find myself expecting to see him somewhere.

There are days, still, that I just can't believe this is real!!

Everyone else is sending their kids off to college. That's what we should be doing. That's what I want to be doing. I guess you just can't have everything the way you want it.

Roger is on the phone right now with a neighbor talking about working cattle, and I just had the most incredible memory of Michael. When Roger was laid up with a broken leg a few years ago, a neighbor was over visiting and was talking about getting help rounded up to work some cattle. Michael was in 8th grade. I remember Roger telling him before he left – if you need some help, just call, I'll send Michael right over! And he did! Michael was so capable of doing anything out here! Anyway, it was a good memory tonight.

God's blessings to everyone.

Friday, August 25, 2006

It's definitely good to be busy. I've kept myself swamped at work this week, and in return, I've had no major "break-down" moments. There have been a few times that I heard a song, or saw something that brought up our new reality of "life without Michael," and I've shed tears, but was able to compose myself fairly quickly. I have thought to myself so many times – I can't cry anymore because there can't possibly be any tears left. But, there always seem to be at least a few. I'm glad to have the days/weeks when there are only a "few," as compared to the "many," or "constant."

The guy from the radio station sent me a copy of the program he's going to air, where he interviewed me about Michael's death. It also included an interview with a father from Sioux Falls who lost his son just a few days before Michael's accident.

I listened to it tonight, and it was kind of hard. I asked Roger and Matt if they wanted to hear what I said, and they said yes. So I played it again, and as soon as it was done Roger just got up and walked away. I asked if he wanted to hear the other guy and he just said no and left. He hasn't said anything since. I'm not quite sure if he liked what I said, or if it just brought back memories that made him sad, again. I'm not completely sure he's ok with my speaking out the way I do.

Again, I said in this interview that we are prime examples of parents who told our son that if you drink, just don't drive. And it didn't work. Michael drank. Michael drove. Michael died. And it all started with "Michael drank."

The other parent who was interviewed talked about starting a foundation that will make available, people that kids can call to come pick them up if they're too drunk to drive. I wish him well, and I hope it saves some kids' life. But I just can't condone that attitude anymore.

I know for a fact, and so should everyone else, that a person's mind does not think rationally when they've been drinking. Man, that just seems so basic now! Yet, it took me burying Michael before it meant anything to me. So, I can't blame other parents who still don't understand. I just pray so much that someone else will be smarter than I was, and will understand before they're child dies.

People say that "we did it, and kids are just going to try it." I'm going to try my best to change that. I don't believe that things can't change. The only way things will never change, is if no one ever tries. When someone thought about inventing a car, they didn't say – oh, it can't happen. They said – we're going to try – and it happened. When someone thought about flying to the moon, they didn't say – oh, it can't happen. They said – we're going to try – and it happened. When someone thought about inventing the internet, they didn't say – oh, it can't happen. They said – we're going to try – and it happened. I'm saying – I want to try to convince kids to not drink, period, because it's very dangerous and life threatening. It'll never happen if someone doesn't try.

With the blessing of God, I will do His will.

Sunday, August 27, 2006

Last night Matt was involved in a roll-over accident. Thank God, he's ok, other than some bruises and scrapes. But they sent him to the hospital anyway, just to get checked for sure. I didn't handle it well.

Yes, alcohol was involved. The deputy said he blew a .01 on the breathalizer, or the equivalent of about one beer. Still, there is a zero tolerance in the law for minors to drink.

I just realized that I can't keep trying to speak out, when I can't even get the alcohol controlled in my own house. Matt is the child I never thought this would happen to, especially after what happened to Michael.

If having your brother die in an alcohol accident isn't enough to wake you up and not do the same, then I'm at a loss. I don't know now what it would take to make kids stop. But I know that what I'm doing isn't working, at least at home, and that's where it's got to start, as I've been told so often.

I was never so afraid in my life as I was last night when we arrived and saw the police sirens and ambulance, and the pickup laying on its top, and Matt in the middle of the whole thing. I knew I never should have let him leave the house. Yet, once again, I was wrong, and failed. Thank God, at least this time I'm not planning my child's funeral. But I can't take that chance any more. I have to do something different, but I just don't know what it is.

I've told Roger before that no more alcohol will ever be allowed in my house. He's had a little problem with my taking that stance. He has told me that maybe the neighbors won't want to come help us when we brand or work cattle if they can't have a cold beer when the work is done. He has also said he doesn't think its wrong for him to have a cold beer once in a while after he comes inside from a long, hot day working in the hayfield.
He's right. But I have to go with my heart.

Dear God, please carry me now!

Tuesday, August 29, 2006

Sunday morning, after Matt's near-fatal accident, I got dressed to take him to town for his twice-daily sobriety test, which we will have to do until his court date in nearly three weeks. Anyway, I reached deep into my jeans pocket, which I never do, especially when I know there are no keys in there, and in the bottom was a single dime! I've heard of the "dime story" and know people who have said it happens to them. (A loved one who has died, somehow leaves dimes in strange places that their loved ones find, at just the right moment, to remind them that they are watching out for us.) I didn't think too much of it that morning.

Monday morning at work, I was seriously ready to quit my job. My boss, Tim, was coming over to the office to talk to me about it. I had gone outside the office, over to the bank, the post office, the grocery story – probably six times that morning. The last time I went out, I saw a dime laying on the ground right in front of the door! I told Tim about it, and before he left that day (convincing me not to quit my job), he handed me a dime. Then – when Matt and I were on our way home that evening, I wanted to take him with me to the cemetery. We stopped there, and right on the very top of the gravesite was a dime! It was wonderful!

I told the story to Matt and Roger tonight, and about the dimes I had found. Roger just shrugged it off. Matt turned the tv on. I asked them if they thought I was crazy, and they both shrugged

131

and said they didn't know. I know they think I am. But just wait until they find a dime!

Sunday morning, I had to ask Matt what in the world made him drink a beer the night before, given what we have seen it do to our family. It was obvious he didn't want to talk about it yet. But I persisted, and what he told me made me shudder with sadness and guilt.

He said that all summer long, he tried to have fun with his friends, but just couldn't stop thinking about Michael. He said that night, his friends had the beer, and he thought if he just had one, it might be enough for him to forget about the loss of Michael for just one night, and he could have fun.

Oh, I have a lot of work ahead of me – to heal myself, and help my family heal too.

Tuesday, August 29, 2006

(Reprinted with permission from the Mellette County News – Prairie Ponders editorial column)

Each week I journey through the federal court logs, searching for cases referring to individuals residing in the Mellette and Todd county areas. I came across a case this week that caught my attention. It had nothing, that I could see, to do with our area of South Dakota, but something about it really stood out.

The case was heard in a Rapid City courtroom, and the defendant was from Georgia. He had pled guilty to a charge of Interstate Transportation of Unlawfully Taken Wildlife. Apparently, sometime in the fall of 2004, this individual had "unlawfully transported a mule deer, a white-tailed deer, and an antelope from South Dakota to Georgia in violation of a number of South Dakota state hunting regulations."

He pled guilty to three counts of illegally transporting wildlife across state lines, and was sentenced and ordered to pay a $3,000 fine, $5,000 in restitution to the South Dakota Game Fish & Parks, and $75 to the Victim's Assistance Fund.

Initially, I didn't have a problem with this person's fine and conviction. Then I started comparing it to other crimes.

I've had a concern about adults (anyone over the legal age of 21) who buy alcohol for kids (anyone under the age of 21). Lately, or more specifically in the past three months and 13 days since the death of our 18-year old son in an alcohol-related car accident, that concern has taken a new, more pronounced spot in my daily life.

I've noticed that when an individual who has been charged with Contributing to a Minor actually makes it to the point of a court hearing, the charges are often dismissed or reduced. If by some odd chance the charges hold, I've rarely noticed a sentence of more than 30 days in jail, usually with nearly 30 days suspended. That means they don't have to serve the time. A common fine is usually in the area of $100 to $200, of which sometimes it is also suspended.

So here I sit looking at the scales of justice. Apparently, the value of two deer and an antelope in South Dakota, when transported illegally, is approximately $8,075.

And the value of a young person's life, ruined, or lost, due to an adult contributing the alcohol which made it impossible for the child to reason and be safe, is around $100.

Could someone please, again, explain justice to me? I'm afraid I just can't comprehend it anymore.

Wednesday, August 30, 2006

I went to a joint City Council and Commissioners meeting tonight, where they were discussing their enforcement agreement. One particular city councilwoman was very outspoken. She thinks we have too much law in the city/county, and she thinks alcohol is just fine. I can't even begin to write all of the nasty things she said to me. I spoke up too. And my comments weren't accepted very well, other than by another parent who was there, also speaking up. I walked out of the meeting when she, sagain, said to me that it all starts in the home and that parents should take better care to keep their kids from drinking alcohol.

I cried all the way home. My heart was racing. I couldn't even drive more than 45 miles per hour.

I could actually fell my heart pounding, and I wondered if that's what it feels like when you start to have a hart attack. That happens quite often lately. There is a part of that is just daring God to let me die from a heart attack, right now.

Sometimes I feel so helpless and hopeless, that I would welcome death. I feel like such a failure as a mother, wife and daughter, that I don't think it would matter to anyone in my family at all. I just get so very tired, that I don't want to try anymore. And I don't mean tired because work is too hard, or that I'm physically tired. It's that I'm tired of trying.

Dear God, I need you with me now!

Thursday, August 31, 2006

Today was hard. People called and came in, all about the meeting last night. People must think I'm a total basket-case, for as much as they check on me. Maybe I am that much of a basket-case!

It makes for long days now – with Matt having to take the breath test each morning before school, and each evening. We usually don't get home until 8 p.m., and we've left in the morning before 7:30 a.m. I'll be glad when he goes to court in two more weeks. He seems very ashamed and embarrassed by what he did, and what happened to him. It's more punishment than I could ever give him.

I went to the school today and talked to the senior class. I was going to talk to the whole high school, but Matt said under the circumstances he would like it if he didn't have to be there. I told the seniors that if they kept themselves alcohol-free until they graduate next spring, I would give each of them $100. Roger thinkgs it's silly. He doesn't think they will do it. But I have to try something.

By the time I finished talking to them, every single one was crying, including me. They're not my flesh and blood kids, but they're my "kids." They are Mike and Matt's friends, and I want them to be safe. It's enough that Matt lost a brother. I don't want him to lose a friend too. There are 27 seniors this year, and I hope I have to get 27 hundred dollar bills for them next spring. Someone said that's a lot of money, and I just said it's completely worth it if 27 young people in our town stay away from alcohol for at least the next nine months, and live to talk about it.

Chapter 5

September 2, 2006

Last night was the first football game of the season. We lost. It was sad.

At one point I looked over at the sidelines and saw #82. Michael was #82.

Matt was benched fo the game last night – punishment for violating the school's training rules by drinking last weekend. I think Matt is already doing better. Just the talks we've had seem to have opened him up more. It will continue. It has to. He has to be ok, whatever it takes from me.

A friend told me that writing in my online journal was a way for others to get help themselves as they grieved, by talking to me. It made me want to continue, to try to help others. But I couldn't go on. That online journal had become too overwhelming and exhausting. I need some space, and quiet from people and the world in general. I don't intend to just hide away, although some days I'd really like to, but I need to be a little more "alone" for a while, and "alone" with just my family.

Things have worked out so that I will be taking a two-week vacation from work starting next Thursday. I hate to admit it, but I'm excited. I'm looking forward to some peace and quiet from that part of my life too.

Jim came over this afternoon and helped Roger and Matt move some cows home. He stayed quite a while tonight, and we spent a lot of time talking about Michael. After he left I told Roger that it was one of the best conversations I've had in months. I said the same things I've been saying to other people, but for some reason it felt calm tonight. I don't know if it's because Roger was there also, or a combination of the two of them. Jim is just like family. He's just like a brother to Roger, and he's been just like an uncle to our kids. He went through a very difficult time a few years ago when his mother passed away, and Roger thinks it felt good to talk with him because he knows how we feel. I'm so glad he came over!

I found some pictures on the computer tonight that I had forgotten about. They were from a family dinner we had the night before Michael's graduation. Once again, I felt like he was looking right at me, right now. I wanted to scream out to the world – see, he's not dead, he's right here, looking at me!

I had a long talk with God today. One of Michael's rodeo magazines came in the mail the other day, and I usually avoid them now. But this afternoon I decided to take it into his room and look through it. Shouldn't have done that.

I laid on Michael's bed and started praying. I begged for forgiveness for every sin I could think of. I asked God why he is punishing me so. What did I ever do to deserve this wrath from Him? And now, this punishment of losing Michael that can never be atoned for. Nothing I can ever do will bring him back or make my life better. Nothing physical, at least.

What I have to do, is remember to always praise God for all He has given me; give Him all the glory for what I have, including all I've had with Michael. I guess I should be grateful I had him 18 years. If not for the grace of God, I would never had had or known Michael.

I was able to skim through the magazine, but by the time I was done praying, I didn't have much concern about the news in it. I had broken down again, feeling sorry for myself. I know I have to stop that, but I just miss Michael so terriby much, and my life seems so empty without him.

When you have a second child, you make room in your heart for him/her, and the same with a third child. I think you're heart just grows and grows with each addition. But when one is lost, your heart doesn't shrink back down. It just stays there, with empty space. Sometimes when I feel my heart pounding, I think that must be why. I have empty space in it, and the blood doesn't know how to flow through it any longer. People have no idea how right they are when they talk about someone having a broken heart. I don't think of it as just a saying anymore. It's real. It's as real as your child in a grave.

September 3, 2006

Today while we were having lunch, we talked a lot about Michael. We, including Roger, talked about being mad at him for drinking and driving. Roger said he was made at him right at first, but has gotten over it now. Matt sounds like he's still kind of mad, but not quite as much. We talked about what we would have said to Michael if we had know he was going to die in a few hours, and if we knew we couldn't stop it. We all agreed we would have told him how much we love him. I told Matt and Roger that if I die in a few hours, I want them to know how much I love them right now!

We also talked about salvation. I point-blank asked both Roger and Matt if they believe. Of course I knew the answer; we've talked about this before. But I don't think it ever hurts to reaffirm. They both said yes, and I told them how terribly important it is to know – to know for yourself, and for your family to know about you.

Later this afternoon, it was really quiet for a while. Roger had gone outside to check on the cows and calves they moved yesterday. I checked in Matt's room and he was sound asleep on his bed! Matt wasn't up late last night, and he didn't get up at the crack of dawn this morning either. He hadn't spent the morning doing a lot of physical work. But yet he slept for over three hours this afternoon! I honestly can't remember the last time he's done something like that!

I think he's been exhaused; exhausted with grief and guilt over his feelings, and guilt from the accident he was in last weekend. I truly believe that the talks we've had the past week have alleviated some of that from him. I think his body finally released some of that this afternoon, and allowed him to sleep. I'm so thankful! Maybe, just maybe, he's on his way to finding it a littler easier to accept Michael's death.

Last night when Jim was here, I was telling him how I feel like everyone is trying to put words in my mouth, especially with these messages that say "don't drink and drive." He asked me if I felt like I was being used. It was like an epiphany! Yes, I feel like I've been used! I want to say my words, not anyone elses. I want to believe my beliefs, not any elses. If no one likes what I say or believe – fine. They don't have to listen. But they can't keep using me to spread a message to kids that I believe is the wrong message. I have a meeting this week with South Dakota's Attorney General. I plan on saying that to him, and the radio stations – what they have me saying has got to stop, or change, period.

I watched a movie today – a true story about a little girl who was abducted, raped and murdered. It was days before her body was found. I have been thinking that losing your child is the worst thing on earth that could ever happen to you. After watching that movie, I think now that having your child brutally murdered, or not being able to find your child, has got to be worse. My heart aches tonight for every parent who has gone through that. It makes you realize that as bad as you think you've got it, there is someone out there who is hurting worse.

I was told tonight that it's time to move on. Could be. Actually I think I am moving on. Every day that I get out of bed, I'm moving on. I don't usually want to, because my body aches with sorrow. You don't just bury your child and move on because the calendar say's it's been three months, seventeen days and eight hours since he died, and that means it's time.

September 4, 2006

Today Roger did something I didn't think he was ever going to do. He took what alcohol we had in the house – seven bottles of wine and nine cans of beer, and threw them in the dump! He said that he got madder and madder each time he threw one down and broke it, but that it felt good. He said he was so mad at those cans of beer, because that's what killed Michael, and almost took Matt from us recently too!

I'm so glad he did that! I would have like to have gone with him, but I got the feeling he wanted to be alone when he did it. Matt was in Winner today with some friends, and that really makes me think that Roger picked today so he could do it by himself. I

140

hope it helped him; I know it helped me tremendously to know that he's now on the same page as I am about alcohol!

September 5, 2006

I did a search tonight on the internet tonight, for the name Michael Glynn. It's amazing how many of them there are! It was actually fun to read about many of them. One was even a South Dakota Legislature in 1872 – a relative! Who knew!

Yesterday I found some of the newspaper clippings, report cards and certificates of Michael's. I hope to get them all scrapbooked next week. The very first page is a picture of Michael riding a sheep in Frontier Days when he was five years old. I told Roger – if we only knew that 13 years after that first ride, he would win the bull riding at Frontier Day, and the very next year they would be giving a memorial belt buckle to someone in his memory. I guess it's a good thing we don't know.

I also found a notebook that Michael had written some notes on. It was nothing important – just notes to Roger about checking cattle and things like that. But it's his handwriting. I feel so attached to it. He will never write anything again. It seems silly that things like that would be so meaningful, but they are.

September 8, 2006

Today is the second day of my vacation. Yesterday I spent the day in Pierre visiting with Attorney General Larry Long. I wanted to talk to him about the laws and punishments given to people who buy alcohol for minors. I found out a lot!

He told me that it's usually hard to convict someone of buying for kids. He seemed shocked when I told him that one of the people who bought for the seniors had admitted to it within a week of Michael's death. Of course, it was because he had bought a keg, and they have to be registered to the buyer so his name was on record; and the keg was found at the party site. He advised me to go ahead and talk to our state's attorney about it.

Yesterday I actually bought groceries. I mean, the kind of groceries that you have to cook; not the heat and serve kind! I kept going down the aisles thinking, Mikey like this, and Mikey likes that, I should get this or that for him. But I didn't have to.

I bought a can of peas. I haven't bought peas in years! My kids don't like peas, other than those fresh from the garden, so I never buy them.

When the kids were little and I had a huge garden, I could never can or freeze my peas. The kids, while playing outside, would raid my garden constantly! It was like a pantry for them while they played. They seldom came in the house for a snack; it was all outside. They would dig carrots to munch on, pick ground cherries, rhubarb, even watermelon and muskmelon. But they loved peas from the garden the most. They would go to the garden and eat those hard, uncooked peas, straight from the pod. But they wouldn't eat them after they had been cooked! By the time they got through, I never had many left to can or freeze for later anyway!

I don't really know why I bought that can of peas. I love cooked peas. But I have this feeling I'll never cook them. Maybe I bought them just to look at, and remember a good memory of Mikey, Amber and Matt.

September 9, 2006

Last night Matt broke his arm in the football game. Barely into the first quarter, and he had to block a 276 pound kid. Matt weighs 150, soaking wet. Matt made the block, sending the other kid to the ground, but the other kid landed on Matt's arm. His wrist twisted, and it broke. So we spent another night in the emergency room at the hospital.

While Matt was on the table waiting for the doctor, I started picking little pieces of grass off his clothes and socks. Instantly, it reminded me of doing the same thing to Michael at the Rosebud Hospital. Will I ever be able to have a thought without Michael in it?

I got my answer today. I think it's no. We vaccinated calves, and of course Matt couldn't help. But he was bored stiff in the house, so I drove him down to the corrals so we could watch for a while. The guys were just sorting the heifer calves, and for a few minutes some of the calves wandered into a pen that had an old pile of straw in the middle.

When we were there taking Michael's senior pictures, I saw that same pile of straw and told him to go stand by it for a photo. He got sassy and said, "what do you want me to do, hug it?" Then he put his arms around the top of the straw and I snapped a picture. Then he said, "do you want me to kiss it now?" And he reached down and grabbed some in his mouth, smiling and grinning from ear to ear.

It was so much fun! It was silly, and ridiculous, but we were all laughing. Michael could turn almost any situation into a comedy. It was a good memory, and it was only one month before he died.

It is so hard to go back and remember the one months, the one week, the one day before his accident. You just have no idea what will happen. They say it's good we don't know the future, but wow, do I ever wish I could have know. I would have said so much more to him. I would have done so much more with him. I would have protected him so much better than I did.

September 11, 2006

I keep asking God, what did I do that I, and my family, deserves to have this kind of tragedy in our lives? Why are these things continually happening to us? Between Michael and all of his injuries last year, then his death, and Matt's broken wrist last winter, and now a car accident and a broken arm this year – what are you trying to tell me? Am I so blind that I can't see what this all means? Or are you still testing my faith? I do still have faith. I couldn't survive without it. Just what is it I should be doing with my life differently than I'm doing now? Why are these things still happening to my family? How much more do I have to endure? How much more "can" I endure?

September 13, 2006

Today Matt had court.

September 15, 2006

I keep picturing the courtroom the other day. It was not good. Social Services has to investigate us because Matt is potentially a "child in need of supervision." It seems laughable! The judge told him that the maximum penalty he could face would be removal from our home and placed in foster care! Seems like it should be a joke! It won't happen, but wow, the hoops we have to go through now – ridiculous. We have to fill out a huge book of forms, as does Matt. He has to go to an alcohol evaluation (waste of time for what they do there), and we have to meet with the court's family services people to basically prove that we're fit and are not neglecting Matt.

I wonder what they'd think if I told them what I really feel? What would they do if I told them I probably am neglecting Matt because I can't do anything without thinking about Michael? What if I told them Michael's death was my fault because I should have been a better mother to him? Where were they then? Why didn't they intervene and threaten to take Michael out of my home for his own protection? What if I convince them that I'm a good mother to Matt, then something happens and he dies too?

People keep telling me that I can't keep Matt locked up at home, and I don't. But I sure want to. I don't ever want him to be out of my sight. When he drives to school by himself in the morning, I can't wait until half an hour after he should be there; then I know nobody is going to call and tell me he didn't make it to school. When he comes home, I sit on pins and needles after he's called to say he left town, waiting anxiously for Goldie to bark, knowing that it means he's less than a mile from home.

Life Source called today again. I told the lady something I haven't said to anyone since Michael died. I regret not staying with him until the very second they took him to surgery for the organ retrieval. If I had that to do again, I don't care how tired and exhausted I was, or if anyone else thought I should or not, I would have stayed with him. I would have used those last few hours touching, holding, feeling him.

We also talked about the man who received Michael's heart

and the letter he wrote to us. It is one of the most treasured letters we will ever receive!

September 17, 2006

Four months today.

Last night I ended up sleeping in Michael's bed. I woke up this morning from a dream I was having. Michael's best friend was at our house and I was cooking spaghetti. It was in our old house out here on the ranch – the one we haven't lived in for over ten years. But we were all the age we are now. Anyway, we were waiting and waiting, and finally Michael walked through the door. We hugged and kissed him. He said he had been in prison for the past year and was just coming home for the weekend to visit. All of a sudden a judge walked in the room, and he started telling her how much he had grown up. She told him he didn't ever have to go back to prison. So we all sat down to eat the spaghetti and celebrate. That's when I woke up. That dream must have had something to do with Matt being in court the other day. It wasn't a "wake up in a cold sweat" kind of dream. It felt so real to see Michael – and for whatever reason he had been gone, I was happy.

I felt such a desire tonight to know just what Michael's doing in Heaven. I mean, we really don't know. We know it's perfect, and beautiful, and unimaginable. I have to quit trying to imagine. God tells us that we shouldn't even spend time trying, because it's way beyond our ability. No matter how hard we try, we won't be able to know.

It's just so hard to let go of the nurturing that you do as a mother. It's not like turning off a water faucet. I'm finding that it takes a very long time to let go when your child dies. Yet Michael's death was exactly like turning off a water faucet. One second there was life, the next there was none.

September 18, 2006

A couple of my friends have talked about "windshield time" and how much they love it. It's the time you're in a vehicle, driving, and have lots of time to just think. I hate it. It gives me too much time to think.

Roger and I went to Rapid City today. I love going there with him because he drives, I sleep, he chauffeurs me around, and it's usually very relaxing and fun. We had a great day, except for the windshield time. It was a beautiful fall day and the scenery was goreous. Michael would have loved a day like today.

We had a good talk when we stopped for lunch. I asked Roger if he remembered what yesterday was. He did. It was the fourth month anniversary. I asked him if he felt any better, or if things had become easier for him in the last two months. Without even hesitating he said no. I agreed, completely.

I told him more details about my conversation with the lady from Life Source and how I wish I hadn't left Michael Tuesday night when the nurses made us leave. Then the water works started, right there in the restaurant.

So, we started talking about Michael and what a free spirit he was. Roger and Michael used to eat at this restaurant often when they were in Rapid City, and Roger started reminiscing about his favorite meals there. Strange – what we remember now.

On the way home I kept searching in the clouds. For a while after he died I felt comforted by watching the clouds – like he was there in them, watching me. But today was different. I felt like I was searching and searching, but just couldn't find him like I used to. Maybe it was just the day. Maybe they were just the wrong kind of clouds. Maybe he's just not there.

September 19, 2006

I did something last night that I haven't done for quite a while. I watched the video in memory of Michael that was shown at his funeral. For the first couple of week, I watched it every single night. It got to the piont that I was able to smile when I saw the pictures. Last night it wasn't that way at all.

I went into Michael's room then. I took the deer antlers down last week and put them in the hunting room downstairs. That one little thing missing, made the room seem so much barer last night! I've been keeping the door open most of the time too. Michael's smell has virtually left completely, so I haven't seen the point in keeping the door closed. I don't want the room to become a shrine, so I've been trying to ease myself into making it "just another room" in the house now. I laid down on the bed and wrapped Michael's comforter around me, and I couldn't believe it – his smell was in there, in the blanket, and it was overwhelming! I just lay there with it wrapped close, and cried and cried and cried. I was so thrilled to have that smell back! Then I got mad.

I got mad thinking that this is all I have left of Michael – a bunch of pictures and a stupid blanket that smells like him once in a while. It's just not enough. I want more. I need more. And this is all I will ever have.

September 23, 2006
We've had over two inches of rain in the past two days; more than we've had all summer long. I keep thinking today about Michael being buried in a grave. I know it's only the shell of his body that is there. But I can't hardly stand the thought of him being there in this cold wet weather. And winter is going to be here shortly. With it will come the freezing cold and snow. I just see, over and over, his body lying there, covered with snow. He doesn't even have a coat on! I know this sounds really stupid, but I've spent 18 years making sure he had a coat on whenever he went outside in the cold. Now, for the first time, he doesn't have one, and I can't give him one, and it wouldn't do any good if I could put one on him. It's just his body, because Michael is dead.

Then I stood at my kitchen sink and the most wonderful feeling came over me. The rain had stopped, and although there were dark gray clouds in the blue sky to the south, the sun peeked through them in the west. The brilliance of that light as it shined on the wet grass and trees, against the dark colors to the south, was absolutely breathtaking! All I could do was smile and think, man, I wish Michael could see this!

Then, instantly, it occurred to me – Michael is seeing this! He can see it all now! And if I think it's beautiful from here on earth, well, the view from Heaven must be awesome! That's the view

Michael has now, and will have through eternity. It gave me a real warm fuzzy feeling!

Thank you God, for giving me this moment of peace and comfort!

September 24, 2006

I'm listening to *Headin' to the Rodeo*. I remember all the times Michael listened to it in his room while he would thumb through a magazine. He could lay on his bed for hours, listening to music – usually Colby Yates, Hank Williams Jr., or Chris LeDoux, while reading word for word the contents of the latest *PBR, Pro Rodeo Sports* or *Outdoor Life* magazine.

I can picture how excited he would get when it was deer season, or when the boys would call in a coyote while hunting. He thrived on our ranch. He knew every square foot of it – and had been on every inch. He knew every tree and bush. He knew every draw and every hiding place of deer. He knew cattle trails, and where to look for hidden calves.

I wonder if these are things others will remember about him? Or if they will only remember him as the kid who died from drinking too much alcohol and driving?

Maybe it shouldn't matter to me. After all, he was my child, not anyone elses – well, other than Roger. What should I care what other people thought of him? I knew him better than anyone other than God. I knew him as only a mother can. I knew what kind of a person he was. I knew his faith. I knew his heart. I know he's ok. I know – and that's really all that does matter.

September 26, 2006

Roger went out to replace the cement around a water tank in one of our corrals today. He noticed that in the cement was Michael's handprint and name, from when Roger and Michael put that tank in several years ago. He said he couldn't tear it up then to replace it. He'll have to figure out a way to fix it and not ruin Michael's handprint in the cement.

September 28, 2006

Today was payday. We sold our steer calves. It's a good six weeks earlier than usual, but we're running out of grass on the place because of the drought, so they had to go to town. We're hoping that with them gone, we'll have enough grass for the heifer calves for a few more weeks.

We've always let the kids skip school on the day we sell calves. It's a huge event on a ranch. The cattle market that one day dictates if we'll be able to pay off our loans of the previous year, and what kind of a start we'll have towards living expenses for the next year. So we take it pretty seriously. And since the kids play a big part in helping with the work out here, we feel they deserve to be there the day we celebrate the year's work.

When the kids were little, we used to make them take a note-book and pencil with them to the sale barn. They would have to figure the total price of a sale by multiplying the weight by the cost per hundred-weight the cattle brought. It would keep them pretty busy and occupied, and it made us feel less guilty about them missing a day of school.

So, Matt skipped school today to help. Even with a broken arm, he was able to ride to corral the cows and calves, and helped sort and load the calves.

I went down to the corrals to watch the guys load calves. Michael would have been in the back, bringing a few head at a time up to the chutes. While the other guys took the calves up into the truck, Michael would have been telling a joke. He would be having fun no matter what he was doing.

At the sale barn, I looked behind me once and saw a couple with two little boys. Boy, did they give me a feeling of de ja vu. I instantly had a vision of Michael and Matt playing with their own toy cows, horses and tractors at the sale barn when they were that age. A few years later, Michael would be helping the barn owner's daughter hand out buyer numbers, ignoring his little brother. The last couple of years, he just hung around Roger at the sales, learning to be a man.

He was learning to be the man that he never got the chance to be. He would have been a good one, I'm sure. Yes, it was a good day. But it was a hard day.

October 3, 2006

I went to the courthouse, and the rumors I heard at the football game this week, were not rumors. The person who bought alcohol for the seniors at their party, who was caught, and admitted to it, has been in court already – without me knowing. The hearings were waived, and the judge sentenced him then and there, without us having the opportunity to speak, as AG Larry Long said we would be given. On the count of Contributing to Minors Under the Age of 18, he was sentenced to 180 days in jail, but 150 days were suspended. He was given no fine. On the count of Contributing to Minors Between the Ages of 18 and 20 – the one that refers to Michael, who, by the way died – he was sentenced to 30 days in jail with all 30 days suspended, and no fine for this charge either! So basically, he got absolutely nothing for committing a crime which led to the death of my son!

I could hardly wait to leave the clerk's office. I felt like I was going to pass out! Once again, like I do so often, I went back to the office and sat and cried. It's a good thing I work by myself most of the time. If I had co-workers around me, they'd think I've gone mad.

Oh Mikey, I miss you so much I can hardly stand it. My heart isn't just broken, it is completely shattered. I try to gain comfort by focusing on other parents who have lost a child, and I try so hard to believe that they are living and someday I will be able to live again also. I was the only one who could have been your mother, and I'm the only one who misses you this way. No one will ever understand, and no one will ever be able to take my pain away.

I wish I could atone for not keeping you safer, by spending 30 days in jail myself! Instead, I think my sentence is to spend the rest of my life on earth missing you.

October 4, 2006

Tonight we had our first youth group meeting of the year at church. I think it went pretty well. We talked about salvation and just what that means. I referred a lot to Michael and the message Pastor Jackie gave at his funeral. It is not my intent to dwell on Michael or his death at these meetings, but I hoped it would be a good place to start, to get their attention. It definitely got their attention! You've never seen a group of kids who were quieter! I told the kids that the only thing that gets me through Michael's death, is knowing without a doubt that one day I will see him again in Heaven. And the reason for that, is Salvation – knowing and believing in our Lord, Jesus Christ.

October 8, 2006

The moon was very bright last night.

Our bedroom is in the southeast corner of our house, with windows on both of those sides. The curtains aren't much more than shears and the moonshine really brightens up the room. Michael's room, on the other hand, is on the northeast side of the house. Michael liked it dark, so his curtains were very dark and densely woven.

Last night it was just too bright and I couldn't sleep, so I went into Michael's room. It was dark and his aroma was thick. I laid down on the bed and was overwhelmed with the thought of him in a grave. It felt sickening to think of him under the cold, hard ground, in complete darkness.

I told myself that being six feet under the ground isn't that far; I could dig it up by myself. I tried devising a plan to open the vault with an ax or bar. I could just go there right now, start digging, and by morning I could be touching and holding Michael again. I could bring him home and tuck him into his bed like I did when he was small. I'd put plenty of covers over him to keep him warm. Then everything would be right in my world again.

Then, a sense came over me that reminded me it's only his body that is lying in those conditions. His soul is shining in everlasting brightness. His body will sleep forever in the dark, but his sould lives forever in the light – because he believed. And I know this, because I believe. I fell asleep then and finally had a restful night.

October 12, 2006

Matt had to go to court yesterday to finish that process from his accident in August. The social worker met with us prior to court, and she was very nice. After she told us her recommendations, she said we would have the opportunity to talk to the judge. I laughed, out loud! Now we can talk to the judge? Where was our opportunity to do that when the guy was in court that sold the alcohol to Michael?

It had a good ending, I guess. I think the whole thing scared the be-jeebers out of Matt, and I'm glad. I want him to know how serious it is to drink and drive – and to simply drink!

Some days I just can't wait for Matt to grow up and settle down, because then I will be ready to die myself. I just feel like Matt's the only reason I even have for going on with life, and once he doesn't need "mothering" any more, it can just all end.

Do I need counseling? I think the social worker that talked with Matt for the court thinks so. She acted as though we should get family grief counseling. The judge even mentioned it. I was adamant that I would not do it. I just don't see how somebody who hasn't lost a child, could ever begin to know how I feel or know what to say to make me feel better. And for the most part, I don't think even Roger could help counsel me through this. Roger did tell me the other day that he had a talk with Matt, and told him it's ok to cry about missing Michael, because he does it himself, every day. I'm very grateful for that. I think that must have been a powerful conversation!

October 17, 2006

Five months today.

Sunday afternoon we got a call from the monument company, wanting us to meet them at the cemetery so they could erect Michael's headstone. I can't believe how much work goes into that job. It took them over three hours! They were very precise though, and very nice to be around all afternoon. After they were finished, Roger moved some of the dirt to level things off again, and I spruced up the flower arrangements and memorials others have put on Michael's grave. It looks nice. And the headstone is beautiful. We were able to keep the wooden cross that Roger and Matt built in its place, with the headstone right in front of it.

Before we left, I just stood and cried. It still seems so unreal. I remember wondering "how on earth could this have happened." Well, "here on earth" is exactly where these things do happen.

Today I received the transcript from the court hearing/sentencing of the adult who bought at least some of the alcohol for the senior party this year. He said he's gone through hell this whole past summer, missing Michael, whom he called his friend. No, he hasn't gone through hell, and in my opinion he has no right saying he has.

Hell is burying your child. Hell is arranging the plastic flowers on your child's grave. Hell is watching your other children living without an admired brother. Hell is being comforted by a bunch of shirts and blankets that you can't bear to throw away or wash for fear of losing the scent that's in them. Hell is feeling guilty because as a parent you're supposed to take care of your child, and you didn't. Hell is living the rest of your life knowing that you failed.

I know Michael is responsible for his role in his death – he didn't "have" to drink the alcohol. And he paid the ultimate price for it. But the people who bought that alcohol for the kids, knowing they would be drinking it – they need to be held responsible for their role too. After all, they didn't "have" to buy for the kids!

Ok, I've said it. I blame Michael too. I blame Michael. I blame those who bought the alcohol. I blame the law enforcement. I blame every person who has condoned kids drinking. Do I blame my parents for not kicking my butt when I drank? Wait! I think they did a couple of times! Why didn't I learn? Why didn't Michael learn? Will this adult buyer learn? Will Michael's classmates and friends learn? Are kids even capable of learning such things? What is the secret? Why do some kids drink, and some don't? Why do some kids learn, and some don't?

I think I try to blame anyone that crosses my path. And I don't blame anyone more than I blame myself. I want someone else to hurt the way I do. I don't want to be alone in this, yet I very much am. And at the same time, that's ok. I am Michael's mother and I'm the only one who can hurt this way. It's just so agonizing.

October 31, 2006

Today is Halloween, although it didn't seem like it. For the first time ever, I didn't carve a pumpkin or put out any Halloween decorations. For the past few years, Matt and his friends would run around on Halloween while I helped Roger's mom and dad greet trick-or-treaters at their house in town. This year, we didn't even do that. After school and work, we just came home.

Maybe it was not wanting to see a lot of coffins, ghosts, deathly looking monsters and such. I heard an ad on the radio the other day about a spook house that was offering tours. They were proud that it was in a building that was once a real mortuary. They said there were still real blood stains on the floor of the old embalming room. I think I'm more sensitive to those things now, and it made me not want anything to do with Halloween.

Chapter 6

November 8, 2006

From High School to Heaven. This phrase came to me on my way home tonight. For some reason I feel like I just have to remember it.

November 9, 2006

Today was quite a day. It was planned, but when it actually happened it was quite nerve-wracking. Keloland sent a reporter out to do a story about Michael and our family following his death. I think it's going to be good. At least it will be another reminder to kids to not drink – I hope.

The whole taping though, was exhausting. I relived the days after Michael's accicent, and all the feelings we had during his time in the hospital, his death, the organ donation, the funeral, our life after… as hard as it was, it was really nothing new.

November 12, 2006

I was going through all of our deeds and important documents today, when I came across Michael's birth certificate. It reminded me that I hadn't filed his death certificate yet. So it's now in it's rightful place, on the page opposite his birth certificate. There are just so many things a parent should never have to do – like look at their child's death certificate.

Even now, I can look at each of my kids birth certificates, and it takes me right back there to the hospital room when they were born. Now, the same thing happens with Michael's death certificate.

I also found copies of our wills. As with many things, they now need to be updated. It was another stark reminder that Matt is the only one left to someday carry on this line of the Glynn family name and the ranch. All our lives have changed so drastically.

November 13, 2006

Well it happened! When I got home tonight, Roger showed

me a dime he found today (his first)! When he finished telling the story of its appearance, Matt said he, too, found a dime at school today! Those dimes were needed, and the timing of them made us all true believers!

Tonight, Michael's story was aired on *Keloland*. The reporter called me today at work to finalize one piece of information. He said that segments like this are usually three minutes in length, but they decided to make this one five minutes.

Those five minutes seemed like forever! I almost didn't watch, because I started crying when I saw one of the commericals for it at the beginning of the news cast. I looked over at Roger and he was clutching his new-found dime in his hand. I told Roger about a jar that I keep the dimes in that I find. I just don't think they should be spent. They're special. They're a message from Michael and God.

Well, we got through the news program, and it was good. By the time it finished, all three of us were crying. None of us could speak. Roger got up and went to my dime jar, and dropped his in.

I keep thinking now, of how Michael loved to see his picture in the paper, usually riding a bull. When the high school finals were televised a couple of years ago, he was elated. He was on tv riding a bull! Now, tonight, an entire segment of the news was dedicated to him. They showed him riding, being handed his diploma, holding Katelyn at the graduation reception, a bunch of his senior pictures, and finally, of his smashed-up car. It's just not fair. This isn't what he was supposed to be on tv for.

Oh, his life was so full. And his future should have been wonderful. His death just has to have meaning! It absolutely has to make others "think," and then "live!" Everyone's life should be justified. Michael's, it seems, will be justified through his death. I have to make it good. I have to make his life and his memory live, for others.

I keep getting these e-mails tonight, from people who saw the news. They say that Michael is proud of me. But I don't want him to be proud of me! I want him here, telling me how unfair I'm treating him because I won't let him go some place. I want him here, making a mess in the house and leaving it for me to clean up. I want him here, asking to borrow money because last weekend's entry fees overdrew him at the bank. I just want him here!

November 15, 2006

I got a call from the reporter this morning. He told me he received a call from the recipient of Michael's heart. He heard about the story on the news and a friend of his recognized the letter he wrote to us. It sounds like he's a very genuinely nice and thankful man. He gave the reporter his e-mail address so we could get in contact with him. I couldn't wait to share the news with Roger! When I talked to him during lunch, I told him that Steve had been deer hunting this fall, and was grateful to be able to do that again. Roger and I have been feeling bad because Michael loved to hunt deer so much, and it's deer season now, and he's not here. I told Roger that at least Michael's heart was able to go deer hunting this year! Roger broke down on the phone and we just couldn't talk anymore.

But all day, I felt so good! It was just so good to know, for sure, that this person's life has been made better through Michael's death! It's one of those confirmations that something good came from Michael dying. In my efforts to keep kids from drinking alcohol, the "good" isn't that visible. It was nice to feel something good, that was concrete!

I shared this news with the youth group at church tonight. I think it really made them think. Our conversation tonight centered around being thankful. It was a perfect fit, to tie that message in with Steve's thankfulness for receiving Michael's heart, and our thankfulness that he is now healthy!

November 16, 2006

I got an e-mail from a lady today who went to school with Steve, the man who received Michael's heart. She then faxed me a copy of a news article that was written about him after the transplant. It had a photo of him in the article. I read it over, and over and over. He truly deserved to have another chance at life.

What an emotional day, and evening it has been.

November 18, 2006

This morning I got a message from Steve! I couldn't believe it! He wants to know everything he can about Michael, and wants to share with us things about himself. It sounds like he's thought many of the same things we have – basically not sure what to do or say, not wanting the other families involved to be offended or hurt. I am anxious now to meet him. I want him to know just what kind of a kid Mikey was, and what a wonderful, good and strong heart he now has. I hope he lives to be 100 years old!

November 22, 2006

It's Thanksgiving Eve. Six months ago we buried Michael. At 2:15 this afternoon, six months ago, I kissed his cheek for the last time, right before they closed the lid on his casket.

I went to the cemetery today. I was there for a long time. The wind was blowing and it felt good to feel the wind. I cried a lot at the cemetery today. Even that felt kind of good.

Tonight I sent an e-mail to Steve. We're starting to refer to him as "our Steve." I hope he doesn't think that we're stalking him or anything! I told him that we, too, would like to meet him sometime.

I want to have a nice Thanksgiving tomorrow. I feel like I have to try, for Matt's sake. Roger's parents are going to his sister's house, and Amber can't get time off to come home both Thanksgiving and Christmas, so it will be just my parents here with us for dinner. I shouldn't feel like that's not enough. I mean, if Michael were here, it would only be one more person! I suppose it's just the realization of knowing that he will never again sit at the table with any of us for a family celebration or Holiday.

November 24, 2006

Well, we made it through Thanksgiving Day. Dinner was simple, and afterwards we all sat down in the living, and fell asleep – every one of us! Matt even went into his bedroom and slept. It was

158

strange. We normally don't do something like that at all. Usually it's an afternoon of playing cards and games, or doing something outside. I wonder if our sleeping wasn't a way for all of us to make the day go by quicker.

The important thing – we made it through.

November 25, 2006

We started talking about Christmas today, and what we would do without Michael here. My mom has given each of the kids a special ornament each year, depicting something special they have done that year. She already bought Michael's – before graduation last year – a graduation ornament that will hold his picture. I told her we should go ahead and hang it on the tree this year. I asked Roger it he'd be ok with us putting Matt's ornaments on the regular tree (Amber has hers now), and dedicating the kids' little ornament tree of mom's, to just Michael. He said that would be good, then began to cry. Then, of course, I started to cry too.

Roger said if it wasn't for Matt, he'd just as soon not even observe Christmas this year. He said he's very afraid he will break down watching everyone open gifts, with Michael not there. I guess if that happens, we'll just deal with it at the time, like we have to do with everything now.

I think our prayer for Peace on Earth will take on a whole new meaning for us this Christmas. I think the peace on earth we will be asking God for, will be not only global, but for peace in our own hearts as well. Yes, we will be praying for peace.

December 13, 2006

(Reprinted with permission from the Mellette County News – Prairie Ponders editorial column)

Many people have asked me to share with them the steps that we took during and after we agreed to allow our son's organs to be donated. For those of you who are new to the community, or new readers of this column, I'll briefly start from the beginning.

Our son, Michael, was in a car accident the day after his high school graduation last spring. He was taken by ambulance to the Rosebud Hospital, where, after seeing his patient records, I still can't believe he was alive at that point. His blood pressure was almost non-existent.

By noon on the Monday morning of the accident, he arrived by plane at a hospital in Sioux Falls, where we were expecting surgeries and extensive treatment and therapy to begin. However, that was not to be.

Although Michael had no broken bones or external injuries, he did suffer severe and irreversible brain damage, as we were informed the following day. It was also discovered that his spleen was the only internal organ that was damaged.

One day later, Wednesday afternoon, after two and a half days of hoping and praying for a miracle, Michael was pronounced brain dead.

At the end, when we were informed of the results of the final tests which confirmed his brain death, we were asked if we had considered donating his organs to others in need. At the time, we were so numb and in shock, that it would have been very easy and understandable to simply say no. But we took the time to have them explain what organ donation would entail. It was time well spent and extremely non-regrettable on our part.

A new team of nurses came to talk with us. These people represented our area's organ donation organization, called Life Source. They said it was important for us to know that they were completely separate from the hospital staff, and that they were only called to talk to us once the determination of brain death had occurred.

We were told, first of all, that at any given moment, over 93,000 people across the nation are on waiting lists for life saving organ transplants.

We were informed, one by one, of each organ and body part that we might consider donating for transplant. I remember being surprised that things like skin from a person's back can be retrieved for transplant in burn victims; blood veins can be used for patients of heart surgeries; even certain bones can be used to enhance other's lives.

There are life-enhancing organs, and there are life-saving organ donations. The life-saving donations include the major organs, of which there are seven - heart, two lungs, two kidneys, pancreas and liver. We could have said yes to only one organ, or any combination of whichever body parts we chose. It was completely up to us. We agreed to allow each of Michael's life saving organs to be retrieved for possible transplant.

Of course, they told us that none of these organs might actually be suitable for transplant, and they wouldn't know this until they operated on Michael to retrieve the organs. If they had been unsuitable, or damaged in ways they yet did not know, they asked if we would agree to allow them to be used in university hospitals for research purposes. We agreed, thinking that once they had gone through the surgical process, the organs should have some purpose; if not to actually save a life, to at least allow medical students to learn from them.

After about an hour's discussion, during which time the people from Life Source asked us to share many, many stories about Michael, and after all of the paperwork was signed, the Life Source team began their real work. They had to search the transplant waiting lists and find suitable candidates for Michael's organs. Once the candidates were chosen, doctors were flown to Sioux Falls for the surgery that would render the organs they needed for each of their specific transplant patients. This work took until the next afternoon.

We were told that because of our decision, they would have to keep Michael on the ventilator, to keep his organs as viable as possible until the scheduled time for the operation. We went back to see him, and say our final good-byes, even later that night. He didn't look the least bit different than he had that morning, and the care his nurses gave him was the same. His body, with the exception of his brain, was there, because of the machines. But we knew his spirit had already been lifted to Heaven.

From the moment we agreed to allow Michael's organs to be donated, the further expenses of his care, including surgery, became the responsibility of Life Source.

We came home the next day - the day his organs were retrieved.

The following day we received a call from Life Source, telling us that a miracle had occurred. Michael's seven organs had all been very good, and had actually saved eight lives the previous night. The doctors were able to divide his liver, giving it to two recipients, one of which was a 10-month old baby. They told us that it is a very rare occurrence when eight lives can be saved from the organs of one person.

A few minutes later we left our house to meet with the funeral home to make those arrangements. It was such a strange feeling - to be so full of pain at our loss, yet so full of happiness at the joy we knew those other eight families were experiencing. Somehow, I believe, it made that trip to the funeral home just a little bit easier to bear.

They call organ donation "the gift of life." But after learning more about it, I think another valuable gift should be that of sharing with your family what you're thoughts are about organ donation.

Many people believe that if you simply mark the organ donor box on your driver's license, it will happen upon your death. This is not exactly true. It only serves as an indication as to your wishes. A person's organs cannot be retrieved upon death unless the next of kin allows it.

So, even if you think by telling them at the Department of Motor Vehicles that you wish to be an organ donor, your family could say no if the opportunity came about. That's why I think it's vital to talk about it amongst your family. Let them know your wishes, so they can honor them upon your death.

Often, in accidents, people die at the scene, or so shortly afterward that it makes it impossible for organ donation to even be an option. For instances such as Michael's, I believe it was God's intention for us to allow his organs the chance to save other's lives. I believe it is why we were given almost three days after his accident to be with him, to tell him we loved him, to say goodbye, and to offer life to those eight other people.

Life Source representatives call us fairly often, just to check on us and see how we're doing. We are allowed to send letters to those individuals who received Michael's organs, but they are screened through Life Source, and cannot divulge private information about us or Michael. The same policy is used for the organ recipients. They can send us letters, through Life Source.

We have only received correspondence from one person - the man who now has Michael's heart. By chance, he found us after friends of his saw stories about Michael's accident in the media. We talk to him through e-mail regularly. We are all trying to be acutely aware of each other's feelings and emotions as we proceed the unfamiliar road of getting to know the person who is alive, only because our son died. It's hard. But it's also wonderful.

Knowing that Michael is spending Christmas, literally, in the arms of the One who is the whole reason for the Holiday, is comforting. Knowing that other families are rejoicing the new-found life of their loved one this Christmas, is also comforting.

I hope that each of you will at least discuss the possibility of organ donation with your family, in the event an occurrence in your life may warrant it. Telling your family that you would like to offer the gift of life to someone else upon your death, may be the most loving gift you could ever give your family.

December 30, 2006

It's been a very long time since I actually sat down to write in this journal. I've wanted to write, and I've thought about the things that I wanted to write, but I just couldn't put them into words on paper – until now.

Finally, the holidays are virtually over. Maybe that's why I'm feeling like I can write now.

After Thanksgiving, came our anniversary. Roger and I went out to supper, and what did we talk about mostly? Well, Michael, of course. When we are alone together like that, he is at the center of our conversations. I personally was thinking about Michael that night, because who knew, 21 years earlier as Roger and I began our married life together, that we would bury a child together.

Now I see young people with their very young children, and I wonder – will they be burying that child in a few years? Sometimes it's almost unbearable to see a young, happy family.

Roger wanted to skip Christmas this year. He was afraid of breaking down in front of everyone. I told him we had to go on with it, at least for Matt and Amber's sake. And if he broke down, we all would, and it would be ok because we're all family. As it turned out, we made it through the day with no major upsets – at least outwardly.

Roger and Matt brought home a Christmas tree, and it sat in our living room for nearly 10 days before I relinquished and decorated it. I guess the closer it got to Christmas, the more I wanted to just agree with Roger, and skip the whole family scene. I had to remind myself, constantly, that Christmas is a celebration of Jesus' birth – not just a time when families are supposed to be together. For the most part, it worked. The tree and house got decorated, and on the 23rd of December I did the shopping.

Around the middle of the month, the funeral home held a remembrance service for everyone who had passed away during the year. We all went to it, except Matt. The funeral home gave each family an angel ornament with their loved one's name and date of death inscribed. We were fortunate to be given a few extra ornaments to share with family and friends.

On December 22, White River played its biggest basketball game of the season. We're rated number one, and we played Faith, rated number two, who beat us at the state finals last year. And – it was a home game. I sat in the bleachers during the B game. All these kids kept coming in and sitting down in front of us – kids home from college – Michael's classmates.

Shortly before the A game, I went down to the floor to get ready to take pictures, and stopped to say hi to some of the kids. The first was Joey. I think he was kind of uncomfortable with me. Then it was Jerod. Jerod was so close to Michael – they had that rodeo bond that no one else in their class shared. They were inseparable. Except that night. Michael wasn't with Jerod. Michael wasn't sitting with all his classmates. Exactly seven months earlier, those same kids were all gathered in the same gym, saying goodbye to Michael at his funeral.

I said hi to Jerod and gave him a hug, and he started to cry. Then I started to cry.

Then I had to leave. I felt like my chest was going to explode. I started to stare at the group of kids, just knowing that if I looked hard enough, I would find Michael in the middle of their group. I kept staring, and he just wasn't there. It was horrible.

I left before the game even started, and spent the next hour sitting in the dark at Michael's grave. It was cold and windy, and it felt really good. Sometimes it feels good to be too cold, or too wind-blown, or even too hot. It dulls my other senses – my other feelings. Being uncomfortable makes the thought of Michael being dead, less painful, if just for a short time.

We've heard from Steve a few times. He seems to be doing very well. The story that was on TV about him was just wonderful. It was so helpful to be able to put a face and a voice with him. I already feel like I know him well. He seems like a very nice person, and that also makes things better. I just can't wait to meet him and his family, but we've had to put it on hold to get through the holidays.

Like I said earlier, we made it through Christmas Eve and Day. We had a lot of company, so Matt had to sleep in Michael's room on Christmas Eve. It only bothered me a little bit – I'm very slowly allowing the room to be something other than "Michael's room." Matt said it was ok with him to sleep in there that night, and I hope it was. Sometimes you don't know about him, because he is so agreeable to anything we ask, and never complains or questions what we ask him to do.

A few people have given us special ornaments this year, to remind us that Michael is spending Christmas with Jesus this year, and special things to help us through the holiday. I put them all on Michael's tree, too, along with the angel ornament from the funeral home's service.

Michael and Matt, and my two nephews have been the four boys in our family – forever. It was so obvious that Michael was gone as we sat at the dinner table. I could feel tension – but maybe it was just me. Then our granddaughter, Katelyn, reminded us gently that Michael was an angel now. Maybe she sensed what I was feeling, and just had to remind me of what was positive about Michael not being there.

We heard from the organ donation team at Sioux Valley hospital. They are being included in a Donate for Life float that is going to be in the Tournament of Roses Parade on January 1. They sent us a gorgeous red velvet rose, and asked our permission to have one (a real rose) in honor of Michael, with a banner showing his name, on their float. Of course we agreed. Now we have to make sure and watch the parade on TV that morning! Just think – Mikey's name will be included in the Tournament of Roses parade!

Chapter 7

January 10, 2007

Today was the day I just lost it for a while. I even yelled at God.

Afterward, I sat here and swore I was losing my mind. I go to bed at night thinking about Michael; I wake up in the morning thinking about him; and I'm consumed with thoughts of him all day long.

I walked aimlessly though the house, just crying and screaming for a while this afternoon. I feel like I'm trapped. I feel like I'll never get out of this maze that keeps me searching for Michael; that makes my mind constantly relive his graduation day, and the days in the hospital; that makes me feel anxious and worried all the time about Matt, fearful that something will harm him too. I just want so badly to forget for a while. Yet I'm also afraid of forgetting. I want to remember every single minute detail about Michael. Even now, at the moment, I'm trying to remember his voice, and some of the things he used to always say, and the way he said them.

I don't want to forget anything. But I also want to forget all of the pain. I can't find a way to do both. This is hard. This is really, really hard. And no one really has a clue, except those who have also had to bury a child. My heart aches for them, in ways I never thought possible.

February 9, 2007

I've sat down at this computer to write something in this journal so many nights recently – and my fingers just freeze and I can't even type. Maybe it's a good sign that I can tonight.

This week, Roger and I met with the Grandstand committee and committed Michael's memorial funds to pay for arena lights at the rodeo grounds. I feel really good about that. Back when the new grandstand itself was built, Michael would go into town with Roger to help. He was so young – 11 or 12 – but he thought he was such a man! They even gave him an appreciation certificate and pin, just like everyone else got who helped.

I remember asking him once, not long after that, what would be the first thing he would buy if he all of a sudden had a million dollars. His answer? Bucking chutes. Of all the things he could buy with that much money – very expensive things – he only wanted bucking chutes. He used to say that he was going to come home after college and raise bucking bulls. Roger used to cringe at that. He's been breeding a very calm disposition into his cow herd for many years, and Michael wanted to bring ornery bucking stock into the mix!

The point I'm making is that Michael loved rodeo. There was no "like" or "like a lot" or "really think it's cool." Michael LOVED it. The Frontier Days rodeo is held the same weekend as a three-performance Little Britches rodeo in Edgemont. The last couple of years, Michael simply refused to go to Edgemont, because he wanted to ride at home during Frontier Days. And the last year of his life, days after just turning 18, he won the bull riding! He loved that arena, and he loved riding in front of a hometown crowd.

Michael loved riding under the lights at night or inside a large arena. He didn't get a lot of chances to do that, but when he did he sure talked about the thrill it gave him. I suppose part of it was making him feel older, and more "grown up" like the pros.

There are certainly kids who could ride bulls better than him, but I absolutely, without a doubt, solemnly know that No One loved the sport of rodeo and riding bulls more than Mikey.

When the new grandstand was finished, Roger said that Michael stood back, gazing at the whole arena, and said the only thing the place needed now was lights.

So, knowing all of this, how could Roger and I not want to give something to future rodeo athletes and fans in White River – in memory of Michael?

Some of the committee members asked if we were sure we wanted to pay for something so expensive ourselves, without any outside contributions. Here is my response: People from the White River community gave a sizeable portion of the memorial fund we have. I don't want to go and ask them for more donations now, to help pay for something that Roger and I personally want to do. I mean – maybe not that many people think it's really necessary to have lights in the arena. We will never have the opportunity to buy Christmas and birthday gifts for Michael, ever again. Nor will we have lots of little grandbabies from him to buy gifts for. So we're kind of considering this as a gift to Michael – one last gift. Every single time those lights get turned on, we'll think of Michael, and I hope everyone else will too.

February 11, 2007

It was a pretty quiet weekend, although last night was the annual Sweetheart Ball. Matt went to it a little earlier than I did. I just wanted to get pictures of the kids for the paper, so went in for the crowing of royalty.

I wanted to get a photo of a few of the candidates whose parents we know well, along with their parents. Even doing this simple and nice little thing, I would look at the three of them standing there smiling, and the only thing I could think of was that Roger and I would never again stand together with Michael. One of the parents kind of joked around about having their picture taken, and I wanted so badly to say – do it, you may not get the chance to tomorrow. But what a horrible thing to even think, let alone say out loud. Yet – that's what I was thinking.

It reminded me of last graduation, when Michael and his classmates got tired of all the pictures, and took off their caps and gowns. I told Michael I wanted one of him and some of his classmates all dressed up in their caps and gowns. But he said they were getting hot. I told him that was okay, and that I would just get them all together sometime during the summer for more pictures. Obviously, that didn't happen.

Will there ever be a time that I don't constantly put the thought of Michael, and not having him here, into every situation?

February 13, 2007

Roger had a bouquet of flowers delivered to me today at work. There were two red roses among carnations and daisies. I know it should have thrilled me, and in one way it did. But in another, it was very sad.

Roger has given me many bouquets of flowers for special occasions, and they've always had three red roses included - one for each of our kids. Last year, there were three red roses, and one pink rose, for Katelyn, our granddaughter. It was the most thoughtful thing he's ever done. So when there were just two today, it just made me feel sad. I'll never have three roses again.

When I got home tonight, I didn't act or seem angry about it, but I asked him why he did that. Well, as it turned out, he actually ordered six roses and the florist just made a mistake. I guess he was trying to break the tradition, too, in a way that might make things easier. I feel so much better, knowing that he wasn't simply trying to eliminate Michael – even by just eliminating a flower.

February 23, 2007

When Matt and I were coming home from town tonight, we started talking about upcoming brandings. A couple of ranchers already have their date spoken for, and some of the kids are getting anxious.

Matt mentioned the old brown boat – Michael's car. It's been pretty well known for the past couple of years as the "branding crew's" transportation! Michael bought the car from a friend who had used it to get to brandings while he was in high school. Michael was proud to own it, carrying on the tradition. He paid $200 for it.

I remember Michael thinking he got such a great deal. I mean, a car for only $200! But it barely ran. He had to get new tires for it, new this and new that, and he put hundreds of dollars into it. I can't even remember how many times it stranded him some place, and he and his friends would have to tow it into town and get it fixed. The trunk wouldn't open, and I think one of the doors doesn't open. There are no keys, and no ordinary ignition. You have to use a screwdriver to start it!

I remember a neighbor talking about what it looked like when they pulled up at his place two years ago. He said the car was riding so low in the back, and the front end was so high, all he could see coming down his road were hats. When it finally stopped, after it chugged a few times, the doors flew open and nearly a dozen kids piled out. He just laughed and laughed, and thought of how much fun those kids were having. They really loved going to brandings. It was not work for them. It was just a really good time! The boys had a lot of fun with that car.

At Michael's funeral, Matt drove the car, leading the funeral procession to the cemetery, and a lot of Michael's friends he branded with were riding along. It's been parked where Michael used to park it out here, ever since.

Anyway, Matt said tonight that he and some of the others were wondering about using it to go to brandings this year. I thought it might be kind of nice, and I think they may have been thinking that it would be a sort of tribute to Michael – like he was still there with them.

I mentioned it to Roger tonight at home, and he was not at all happy about the idea. He said that car was Michael's, and he thought it should stay that way. He said he didn't think Matt or the other kids should be driving it this spring to brandings. I felt bad for Matt, who said nothing. So, we left it at that – for now.

February 24, 2007

In the fall of 2005 when we sold our heifer calves, Roger had 10 head of all black calves on the sale. He debated a long time as to whether he should even sell them. They were out of a high powered bull, and were just exceptional calves. Well, they came in the ring, and the bidding began. They dollared-out at $790 a head, and he no-saled them.

People in the barn were shocked. I was shocked! Roger had said he wanted $800 a head for them, but I thought $790 was so close, he'd just let them go. He didn't. Even in the sale barn café, later, guys who didn't know Roger were talking about the "crazy guy who no-saled $790 heifer calves!"

On the way home, Roger explained to me what his intentions were. He told me that those were 10 very good calves, and if they didn't bring at least what he wanted (and now, it's a good thing they didn't!), he was going to give them to Michael.

When Roger and his siblings graduated from high school, his parents gave each of them 10 heifer calves with which to start their own cow herd. Roger decided to do the same, and these were going to become Michael's graduation gift from us.

We told Michael about it that night, and he was very excited – and very proud!

From the time each of our kids was born, we had given them one or two cows. The money from their calves each year was put away to pay for college expenses. The kids never really saw their calf-money, but it made them feel like a real part of the ranch to have their own cattle.

These heifers, however, were truly Michael's. He would get to do as he wanted with their calves – including keep their heifer calves to increase his herd, or sell all of them each year.

Not only was this gift extremely valuable, but it was extremely thoughtful. I was so proud of Roger for not selling those heifers, but instead giving them to Michael. And I was equally proud of Michael for being so humble and honored at receiving the gift. Although, he did remind Roger that someday he'd be breeding them or their descendents to bucking stock! It was a very good day.

After Michael died, we went ahead and kept the heifers and had them bred this past summer. They will have their first calves this spring.

Today, Roger and Matt brought them home from the winter pasture, to keep them close to the place when they calve. A storm came through, with rain, ice, snow and strong winds. It's a good thing they were brought home this morning, because one was starting to calve early – by about three weeks!. By 1:00 p.m. this afternoon, Michael's first heifer had a calf on the ground – or, thankfully, in the warmth of the calving barn.

So, now, what do we do? These heifers are always going to be Michael's heifers. I don't think I'll feel right about selling their calves and using the money for ourselves. I don't think it would be right to give the heifers to Matt. That might be kind of weird for him – he'll get his own when he graduates, anyway. I guess we've got until fall to decide what to do. But I do know that those have now become very special, and even more valuable heifers than ever before.

February 25, 2007

I hit a milestone today. I changed the sheets on Michael's bed. It's the first time since he died, and I can't remember when I had before then - maybe a couple of weeks. But, I just couldn't bear to wash the blankets or bedspread. His scent still lingers slightly.

Then, Roger and Matt helped me, and we went through photo albums to find each year's picture of Michael from grade school to put in one of those 12-year frames.

Finally, we moved some pictures around on the walls in the house. One picture is quite large – of a bull elk. I've had it out in our entry way, and Roger wanted it in the living room. I asked him why and he said he just really liked the picture. I asked him if he remembered how he got the picture, and he didn't. So I reminded him. It's a great story!

When Michael was probably 10 or 11, the kids were with me in Winner doing some Christmas shopping. We went in to a photo gallery, and Michael saw this picture right away. He just loved it, and really wanted to give it to his dad for Christmas. The problem was, it cost $350. Well, Michael asked me if I would help him pay for it, and it could be from all of us. I agreed, of course. I knew how much money Michael had, and I thought he'd chip in about $100. We got to the counter, and he pulled out a $10 bill. He laid it on the counter and asked me if that would help. He was absolutely adorable! I told him that would be just fine. He was so proud when we gave that picture to Roger! He knew how much his dad loved pictures of elk.

Roger was looking forward to the year he and Michael would go elk hunting in Wyoming. But, that never happened. Roger told me a few weeks ago that he has no desire to ever go elk hunting again now.

March 2, 2007

Tonight, for the first time since you-know-when, I sat down and watched Cowboy U with Matt. Roger has been watching lots of bull ridings on tv; he says it reminds him of Michael. I, on the other hand, haven't been able to watch bull ridings. For me it's been very hard. Well, tonight I know why. I felt like my throat was swelling and I was going to choke. My head started hurting and I felt dizzy. And, I mean, this was Cowboy U! For crying out loud, they are city slickers!

Michael and Matt used to joke around about him getting on the show. He planned how he would apply for it and act like he was a sissy or something, and act like the animals were really scaring him. Then he would get there and win the big cash prize. Then he said that maybe some day he'd host the show. He could have, too. He had the knowledge, the ability and desire, and the charisma.

I happened across a quote today that read – every man makes his own destiny. Why, with all the dreams and plans that Michael had, did his destiny have to be to die? It's because he chose to drink alcohol and get in his car. Well, it's because he chose to drink alcohol – period. I don't really believe that he was in any state of mind, after the effects of the alcohol, to consciously make the decision to drive. It was the alcohol that was speaking that told him he could drive. My God, if there is anything I've ever hated more in my entire life, I can't imagine what it was. The very thought of tasting any kind of alcohol, or someone I love or care about drinking that evil garbage, just makes me ill. It killed my son.

April 18, 2007

(Reprinted with permission from the Mellette County News – Prairie Ponders editorial column)

How many people go to bed at night, and really get a good night's sleep? Do you?

I don't believe I've had a truly good night's sleep in 11 months and 3 days, but for far different reasons than most people. Thank God.

There used to be a time, when as soon as I heard one of the kids' car come over the hill and pull into the yard, I would sigh with relief, and drift off into a deep slumber. Those days are long gone.

Prom is over in White River, and Graduation is just around the corner. Brandings are being scheduled. Spring is in the air, and kids, and adults, are feeling energetic. I hope it stays that way - the energy. The alternative is, well, you know.

I've been doing a lot of talking to kids lately, at schools and various events, as well as talking to them personally. Some friends have told me that it's important to keep reminding kids about the dangers of drinking alcohol, especially this time of year. But how often do people remind each other, as adults, about how to act around our kids?

I've heard too many stories the past few days, some from high school aged kids, about the actions of adults they've witnessed, drinking and making fools of themselves. What bothers me is when adults put themselves into positions of being able to really have relationships with our kids, and act as role models, then allow these same troubled kids to see them in drunken stupors.

Someone asked me last week if I knew of any organizations in the area that are focusing on stopping kids from drinking. My answer was that I don't know of anything organized, but I do know there are people out there trying to lead by example, and show kids there are alternatives to drinking and using drugs.

Then there are those...

I can't think of anyone who hasn't shown compassion and offered sympathy to myself and my family since Michael's death. And many of these people share in our new-found concern and commitment to making sure the same thing doesn't happen to any other kids or families. Then, it seems, there are those who as soon as they're finished talking, head to the bar, or worse, take a bunch of kids with them. I think there are a lot of places that adults could take kids to "chill out and have fun" without being exposed to wall-to-wall alcohol advertisements. Believe me, advertising works well!

Well, if you want to talk the talk, then walk the walk. Stop drinking. Stop exposing our kids to alcohol! Show our kids that you mean what you say when you tell them alcohol is dangerous. Or, don't you really think it's dangerous? Do you think getting into a vehicle to drive when you stagger across the street, or fall on the floor of the bar won't cause danger to yourself, or someone else?

The White River community has been fortunate the past year, in a way. At least, those that I can think of who have died in alcohol related vehicle accidents, didn't cause anyone else's death also.

Personally, I honestly don't know how I could have gone on if Michael would have had someone with him who would have died also, or if he would have hit another vehicle and caused someone else's death.

Our community has experienced a death of a young teenager, and we've seen the death of an older father. So we can't say the fault lies with just our kids. Our adult population, I believe, is not doing enough to stop kids from drinking. And we are where the responsibility lies. We simply can't continue to preach one thing to kids, then do the opposite, in plain sight of them. And we have to do more to stop those who are providing this poison to our kids.

People over the age of 21 and legally considered adults, are buying the alcohol for our kids.

I always seem to hear about the kids who have got caught drinking. But how often do you hear about the adults who bought the alcohol for them? Do the people who provide the off-sale alcohol have any inkling to who some of the kids' buyer's are? I'd just about bet so, but it will likely always be denied. Why? Well it could affect their sales, of course. And making money, even at the expense of other's health and even their lives, must be more important to some.

I was told when Michael died that there were many people who provided alcohol for the kids that night for their graduation party. I was also told that I wouldn't want to know the names of everyone, because it might be too painful for me to know. I was also told that if it were known to the community who some of these people were, it would really shake the community up.

Well, guess what folks. My world is upside down! There are dozens of Michael's friends whose world is upside down! You can't do anything that would make me feel more pain than I do now. And the problem is continuing. There are still kids out there drinking, and adults showing them how "fun" it is to drink, and adults buying them their potential death sentence.

I don't care who they are, I wish I knew who every single person was that bought alcohol for that fateful graduation party last year. I would be after them in court like a lioness.

But for now, since I don't, and probably will never know, at least I can ask this of any adults who still buy alcohol for our kids, or allow them to see you act like absolute idiots, or take them into a bar - how well do you think you'll be sleeping when the kid you buy for is lying in a cemetery? How well do you think you'll be sleeping when your own child is lying in a cemetery?

Don't you dare think it can't happen to you. I didn't think it would happen to us, and yet, here I am - forever sleepless.

Sunday, April 22, 2007

I suppose you could say we're adjusting to Michael being gone. We have no choice. Today marked 11 months since we buried him. Matt left for the state FCCLA convention, so Roger and I wandered the house alone. It was kind of wet and icky outside, so we ended up perusing through photos, and all of Michael's things. I sort of started doing that last weekend, but it was nice to have Roger help today.

It took me nearly 9 months before I could even change the sheets on Michael's bed, so changing other things, and putting things away, has been very slow going.

As of tonight, all of his photos, newspaper clippings, memorabilia and so forth have been sorted and scrapbooked. I asked Roger then, why we did it. I mean, it isn't like Michael will have kids that will someday want to see his stuff. And who knows if Amber or Matt or their kids will ever want to. But, maybe on some

100+ degree summer day, or some blizzardy winter day, Roger and I will get them out and remember.

People keep saying that as we near the 1-year anniversary of Michael's death, that from then on it will start to get better. Well, for anyone who writes books that say that - they are lying. It can't get better. Some days it's very, very worse, even more so than one month after he died.

But - we go on.

I've kept busy lately speaking to some area schools about the dangers of teenagers drinking alcohol. And, I write about it in my editorial column often. I have only heard a couple of people who think I'm going overboard in writing about my disgust of alcohol. But I simply tell them - my speaking out will never bring Michael back. But, maybe my speaking out will keep your child from dying at the hands of alcohol. For that reason, I honestly don't know why they would complain about it.

Graduation is coming up, and this year's senior class and some of their parents have really done some tremendous things in Michael's memory. Theyre having a graduation party at the rodeo grounds in his memory, and donating a metal silhouette to be placed there, of a bull rider. And, they've started a scholarship fund in his memory.

Roger and I are having arena lights installed at the rodeo grounds, and if all goes as planned, there will be a dedication for them on May 5. They have to be up and ready by May 13 - graduation, and the kids' party at the arena - ALL alcohol-free!

I'm not looking forward to the next few weeks, but I plan on keeping myself so busy I won't have time to think too much!

Then, I suppose we'll look back and say - we've made it though the first year, now we'll work on year two.

One day at a time - for sure.

God's graces to all of you!

May 9, 2007

(Reprinted from the Mellette County News – Prairie Ponders editorial column)

Every once in a while, an act of kindness is so profound that it should be a crime to not share the story with others. Our family was fortunate enough to be the recipient of such an act.

It happened nearly one year ago, the day we found out that Michael had been in a serious car accident. He had to be life-flighted to a hospital in Sioux Falls, and only one of us could fly with him. We decided that Roger would go, while Matt and I would drive.

We took a few minutes to stop in White River at the school, and give everyone an update on what was happening. When we headed to the door to leave, a young man was waiting there, and gave me a handful of cash. When I tried to deny it, he told me that I would need it for the trip to Sioux Falls. I tried to tell him that it was okay, I'd get some cash, but he insisted I take what he was offering. He told me all the students had taken up a collection for us. Since I was in a hurry, I didn't spend much time arguing, and just accepted the gift and left.

Matt and I rushed home to pack a change of clothes for each of us and take care of some livestock we had in the corrals.

A few short hours later we found ourselves halfway to Sioux Falls, running low on gas. I stopped to fill up, and realized that the cash this boy had given me earlier was all I had. When I took it from my pocket, I realized it amounted to $150, mostly in large bills. At the time I wondered how a collection from a bunch of kids ended up in these denominations. But, I had more important things on my mind.

During the next few days I spoke with the high school secretary a number of times. I would call to let her know any updated status on Michael to relay to the kids at school. During one of these conversations, I remembered the money that had been given to me, and asked her to find out who all the kids were that had contributed, so I could thank them properly. What she told me then, just made me cry - with gratitude and thanks.

Apparently, after Matt and I left the school the day before, the principal had been thinking the same thing I did hours later. He called this young man into his office and asked him for the names of all the students who had contributed to the cash he had given me. The young man then confessed, telling him it was only his money. He had been to a branding the day before, and had just cashed the check.

When the story was related to me, all the pieces finally made sense.

This boy, then a junior in high school, had seen first-hand the effects a tragedy can have on a family. He had likely witnessed his own parents in many similar situations - rushing to a hospital without giving thought to basic necessities such as cash to buy gas and food.

Wise and caring beyond his years, he passed on the lessons he had so harshly been forced to learn. And in his generosity, he took no credit for himself, but instead gave it to over 100 of his fellow students.

I didn't have the privilege of knowing this young man as a child. He and his family came into our lives and our community just a few years ago. I wish I could have been there, and known them better, when their daughter, and his little sister, passed away after suffering most of her own childhood with cancer. I wish there was some way that I could comfort them, and help to take away some of their pain. But now, I know first hand, how impossible that is for someone to do. Perhaps all I can do, is share this story with those who know this young person. Perhaps it's enough, to let his parents know that they raised a very honorable young man.

I was telling this story to a friend a few days ago, and when I finished, he said, "he's going to be a great person some day."

And I replied, with absolute sincerity, "He is already a great person."

Chapter 8

Thursday, May 17, 2007

Well, here we are – one year later.

I really can't believe we've been without Michael for one whole year. It still feels like it just happened yesterday. I've tried to keep busy today, but I seem to constantly be reliving this day one year ago.

As for this being an abnormally hard day? I think I have prepared myself to believe it would be, but really, it hasn't been. I've remembered and relived certain things, at certain times, on certain days – all in the past year. So in many ways, this is just another one of those many, many days. Today started out exactly like every single other day – I woke up thinking about Michael. And tonight, I'm sure, will end exactly like every single other day – my last thought of the day will be of Michael.

I had a dream a few weeks ago. A good one. Up until now I've only shared it with Roger and a couple of other people. I think it's time to tell everyone.

In my dream, I had died. I don't know how, but I did, and had just met Michael in Heaven. I was so excited, and told him I had been waiting for so long to see him again! He looked at me and said, "but mom, you're not supposed to be here yet, you still have work to do, and you have to take care of Matt." I told him that dad was there to take care of Matt, so now I could be with him to take care of him. Then he told me to walk with him, that he wanted to introduce me to someone. As we walked, I thought of who I'd be meeting. I imagined Michael introducing me to his heroes – Lane Frost, his Uncle Cliff, Chris LeDeoux. Then we stopped, and he said, "mom, I'd like you to meet who has been taking care of me." I looked up, and Michael said, "I'd like you to meet Jesus."

I woke up right after this. And ever since then, I've felt a lot more at peace, and have not had a continual death-wish of my own. Michael is ok.

The last thing I want to share with everyone today, is a poem that Michael wrote last year in school. His teacher just gave it to me yesterday. I think it is awesome, and so "Mikey!"

That Was I
By Michael Glynn

I was that young man you saw
sitting on a high ridge overlooking
the wonders of the western badlands,
Wearing camouflage from my head to toes.
Just sitting, waiting for something
to come running to the cries of the call,
hoping that it wouldn't let me down.

And that was I,
the man you saw sweating so in the shop,
beating, banging on the metal
masterpiece I just crafted.
Hiding behind the mask.
I work away all day
from sun up to sun down.
Piece by piece it all comes together
right there in my hands.
Yes, that was I.

Tuesday, May 22, 2007
    Another milestone today - one year since we buried Michael. It rained here and was even too muddy to drive into the cemetery. I should have just walked in, but didn't. Feels bad to not have been there tonight.
    Yes, time really did stop one year ago. The other day Roger was looking at a flyer for a rodeo coming up this summer, and said he remembered that Michael was there last year. He was there, but it was two summers ago. It's like nothing has moved since last May. Everyone is changing, minute by minute, and day by day, but Michael will stay 18 years old to us, forever. It is definitely a Divine power that still lets the sun rise each day!

God bless everyone.

August 15, 2007

(Reprinted with permission from the Mellette County News – Prairie Ponders editorial column)

"That's the injury that will take his life."

Tears rolled down my face as I heard the doctor say those words to me. Feelings of rage and disbelief overwhelmed me as I was forced to accept the fact that my son was dying.

Then, six months later, the words "Michael's heart is still beating," again brought tears to my eyes, but this time, they were accompanied by feelings of joy and gladness.

There are no words to describe what I felt this weekend, as I was embraced by a man who tearfully whispered, "thank you."

The man, whose name is Steve, is alive today. He is alive because a now 20-year old heart is pumping the life-blood through his 42-year old body. He is the recipient of Michael's heart.

A mere two months after Michael died, we received a letter from Steve, sent rather anonymously through Life Source, the organ donation organization serving the midwest. As per their privacy policies, he was only allowed to tell us his first name, and the state in which he resided.

We knew Michael's organs had saved eight people's lives upon his death, but this was the first, and since then, the only one of those people who contacted us to offer their appreciation.

A few months later, I was asked to tell the story of Michael's accident and subsequent death during a television news show. During the interview, I read the first paragraph of the letter Steve wrote to us.

A high school friend of Steve's saw the news segment and immediately contacted him, telling him Michael's death and our donation of his organs sounded eerily similar to the same time he received his heart transplant. Steve watched the broadcast over the internet, and later told us, "I heard you start to read the letter, and I told my wife – that's the letter I wrote!"

Steve contacted the television reporter, who in turn called me,

183

and said, "Michael's heart is still beating, and I just got off the phone with the man who has it."

The rest, as they say, is history. And this piece of history came full circle this weekend, as Roger and I traveled to Minnesota to finally meet Steve and his family in person.

We told him about Michael, and he told us about his illness. Steve said he has always had a heart murmur, and a few years ago he was required to have a heart valve replaced. He was given a pacemaker, and still, it didn't work. After three heart valve replacements, he was told that over half of his heart was nothing but mush. His wife, Pam, said that he had to literally fling himself back and forth in a recliner to force his heart to continue beating. He was moved to the very top of the transplant waiting list, where his name stayed for nearly three weeks. They waited, and waited, and finally began to plan his funeral.

He told us this weekend, that at 9:32 a.m. on May 18, he received the call. A heart was on its way to the hospital, and he needed to get there right away. Pam said she had to almost push him out the door, because he seemed to be in shock. She said he just sat there and said over and over, "They found a new heart for me."

The transplant was a huge success, and one week later he left the hospital. A week after that he attended the high school graduation ceremonies of his and Pam's two daughters. Since then, Steve said he has continued to become stronger and healthier, with a renewed life.

We've corresponded since last November through e-mail, and tried to plan meeting each other, but it seemed something always came up and we had to cancel our plans. I think maybe, as anxious as we were to meet him, Roger and I were also a little apprehensive. We were a little afraid of how we would react, and how he would react – what we would say to him, and what he would say to us.

When we got out of the car, Steve was standing in the yard with open arms. Any apprehensions we had were immediately lost and forgotten. We all embraced, and we all cried. He must have said "thank you" a hundred times. The words were echoed by his wife and his parents.

We went into the house, and it seemed so easy and natural! They began asking all about Michael. We brought pictures, which we pored over throughout the afternoon. They all wanted to know everything they could about the boy whose heart was giving Steve his breath. And, of course, we loved sharing our memories of Michael!

It was hard to leave. After just one day, it began to feel like we not only became friends, but family. We now have a very rare and unique relationship with his entire family, rare and unique in a wonderful way. Steve is simply a good person. Before we left, they were already making plans to come visit us in the near future.

This weekend reaffirms to us that we made the right decision to donate Michael's organs. Had we not, Steve's family, and possibly seven other families, would likely be grieving today as we are. It feels good to know that through the horrible tragedy of losing our son, another's son was allowed to live.

Steve and Pam asked how we had the frame of mind to think of others while we were saying goodbye to Michael. Our answer to them? There was a higher being than us that made the decision. We were only the instruments who gave the doctors permission. It came from the lessons quietly imbedded in our minds, given us from His Son.

Epilogue

A few months after Michael's death, Roger and I were driving home from somewhere, and as usual, gazing out at the wide open expanses of prairie, made me think of Michael. I asked Roger what he would give to have Michael back. With a shocked look on his face, as wondering how I could even ask such a question, he said, "my right arm... my left arm... my right leg... my left leg... anything." I then asked, "would you give every acre of land, every blade of grass, every cow and every dollar in the bank?" And he replied, "of course – everything." Then I said, "why is it so easy to say we'd give anything and everything to get someone back? Is it because we know it can't really be done? Instead, why aren't we saying we'd give anything and everything to keep from losing someone in the first place?"

That was the moment I knew my life was going to change, again. That's when I decided I had to seriously do anything, give everything, to keep the senseless act of an alcohol-related death of a child, from happening to us, or anyone else, again.

Of course, it didn't happen overnight. In fact, its still, and always will be, a work in progress. But opportunities came to light, and instead of wallowing in sorrow and self-pity constantly, I took advantage of those opportunities.

We formed the Michael Glynn Memorial Coalition during the summer of 2008. In the beginning, it's mission was to provide education opportunities for youth and young adults to stay or become alcohol-free. This non-profit organization has grown substantially since then, and now includes prevention programs in the areas of tobacco and drug use, along with suicide prevention. It has grown into a community organization dedicated to the overall well-being and health of our community, with a strong emphasis on our youth.

A few years ago I was writing a grant for the coalition, and had to include the exact date it was granted official non-profit status. As I opened up the file to the front page of the announcement, reading the date gave me shivers. The official legal date of the

Michael Glynn Memorial Coalition's beginning, was stamped 08-08-2008. I could hardly believe what I was seeing. Remember my fascination with the number eight, and how it related to everything Michael dreamed of in his life – the 8-second bull ride? And now, the organization we formed in his memory, was born on a date full of eights!

The Coalition is growing stronger every year. I believe we are seeing some amazing things happen in our community as a result. Yes, we still have a problem with kids drinking, and adults buying the alcohol for them. But it's getting better. We may be taking baby steps moving forward, but at least we're moving forward.

I've often heard the saying that the only way to guarantee something won't change, is to do nothing. I want a change. I don't want any other young person's life to be shattered like Michael's was. I don't want any other families forced to grieve as ours has. I don't want any other mother to feel the way I do. A very good friend, who also lost a child too early in life, told me that it's a lousy club we belong to – we parents who have buried a child. It's a club in which we don't want any more members.

Today, as we near the tenth anniversary of Michael's death, I look back on what I wrote in my journal the first year and shortly after, and I can't believe I made it through that time. I know families who experienced similar tragedies, and unfortunately they didn't make it through.

I read a letter last night that my Aunt Martha sent me a few months after Michael died. She basically told me to ignore all the "self-help and how to deal with grief" books and messages I had been given. She said my grief is mine alone – it's not Roger's, nor Matt's, nor Amber's, nor anyone elses. It's mine, and I can deal with it in whatever way works for me, with no time constraints. Those were wise words. I've taken her advice many times in my life, with no regrets. This was no exception.

She also shared with me that following Michael's funeral, my dad was visiting with her, and asked how anyone could possibly go through something like this without having a strong faith in

Christ. Also, wise words from a very wise man. I thank God every day that my parents gave me a good foundation from which to build my faith.

There were days that I prayed to God that a truck would hit me on the highway. I didn't wear a seatbelt for months, rationalizing that if I were hit, I wanted to make sure I would die. I didn't want to live with this pain any longer. I was oblivious to what I would be leaving behind – family that I loved dearly. Thank God, He said no to that prayer request.

I am in a much better place now. I want to live. I want to see my family grow. It has been a long, hard road getting to where I am now. There are still days that I don't function the way I once did. There is still a hole in my heart that will never be healed. It just won't. People can tell me from now until eternity that it will heal in time, or some other nonsense. It won't. Only a mother who has experienced the same, knows and understands this. But I'm ok with that. And honestly, I don't want any more mothers to truly know and understand!

I still have days that I cry for no outwardly apparent reason – when I read an old story that Michael wrote, or watch a video of him, or read a sympathy card someone has sent.

But I also have days when I laugh out loud, or smile, sometimes for no outwardly apparent reason – when a kid thanks me for talking to them honestly about alcohol, when another tells me they will never drink alcohol, when a parent tells me they are thankful we formed Michael's Coalition to bring some good out of a tragic event, when I look at a picture of Michael and see him smiling back at me, when the sun shines, when it rains, and when the clouds appear.

I was once asked why I do this now when I'll never be able to stop all kids from drinking alcohol. Most of all, it gives Michael's death purpose. To have no good come his death, would be unbearable for me. So therefore, it gives me purpose too.

I once watched a show on television, where someone had been giving help to a young person addicted to drugs. The young person had been given numerous opportunities for rehabilitation, all of which had failed. Finally, people were telling the helper to just let her go - give up, she can't be helped. He replied by stating that he would never give up, because if he were in that person's shoes, he'd be praying to God that there was at least one person out there who wasn't giving up. That has become my mantra.

And I wonder now, was there someone else out there, who could have interacted with Michael at just the right time, or said some magic words at just the right time, and he would have made the choice to not drink that fateful night, or ever again?

Could that person have been me?

Shouldn't that person have been me?

Will that person be me for some other young person now?

Will that person be you?

∞ ∞